P9-DFN-542

Toward a Rational Society

TOWARD A RATIONAL SOCIETY

Student Protest, Science, and Politics

by Jürgen Habermas

translated by Jeremy J. Shapiro

Beacon Press   Boston

German text: Copyright © 1968, 1969 by Suhrkamp Verlag, Frankfurt am Main

English text: Copyright © 1970 by Beacon Press

The first three essays were published in *Protestbewegung und Hochschulreform* (1969) by Suhrkamp Verlag. The first and third essays were abridged for the English edition by the author. The last three essays were published in *Technik und Wissenschaft als 'Ideologie'* by Suhrkamp Verlag in 1968.

Library of Congress catalog card number: 73–121827

International Standard Book Number: 0–8070–4176–9

0–8070–4177–7 (pbk.)

Beacon Press books are published under the auspices of the Unitarian Universalist Association

Published simultaneously in Canada by Saunders of Toronto, Ltd.

All rights reserved

Printed in the United States of America

First published as a Beacon Paperback in 1971

9   8   7   6

Contents

Translator's Preface

The reader has a right to be informed about the noise level of the translation channel. One way to do this is to comment on some discrepancies between the codes:

1) In current English, "practical" often means "down-to-earth" or "expedient." In the text, this sense of "practical" would fall under "technical." "Practical" (*praktisch*) always refers to symbolic interaction within a normative order, to ethics and politics.

2) Although German has adopted to some extent the corrupt usage of "technology" (*Technologie*) to mean technics rather than its study, the adjective *technisch* means technical and technological. That is, it emphasizes the form of making and controlling as well as the machines used in these processes. It has been translated in both ways. Similarly, *Technik* means technique, technics, and technology.

3) *Zweckrational*, that is rational with regard to purposes or ends, has been translated as "purposive-rational."

4) There are several German words whose extensions are wider than the English words with which they often must be translated. In consequence, important connotations get lost. *a*) *Wissenschaft* means knowledge and science. Because of the English equation of science and natural science, "science" is frequently too restricted a translation and "knowledge" too loose. *b*) *Bildung* literally means "formation," but also "education" and (cultural) "cultivation." In German these narrower meanings always connote an overall developmental process. *Willens-bildung*, literally the "formation of will," has been translated as "decision-making." Given the meaning of *Bildung*, *Willens-bildung* emphasizes the process (of deliberation and discourse) through which a decision was "formed," not the moment at which it was "made."

c) As an abstract noun, *die Öffentlichkeit* literally means "publicity" in the sense of publicness. For obvious reasons, it has been translated instead as "the public realm." But, as a concrete noun, it also means *the* public. Thus its use in German bears a more concrete connotation than the former and a more abstract one than the latter.

d) *Herrschaft* literally means "lordship," i.e. generally "domination," and thus by extension "political power," "authority," or "control." No one of these terms is univocally adequate, especially because of differences between their implicit valuations. In this translation, *Herrschaft* has often been rendered as "political power," but also as "domination" or "authority."

5) It is unfortunate that there is no English equivalent for *Naturwüchsigkeit*, since the concept is of importance for critical thought. Literally meaning "growing-out-of-natureness," the term refers to entities or structures that just develop spontaneously in continuity with what came before, without ever having been subjected to consciously directed human will. It is a concise way of saying *le mort saisit le vif* (the dead seizes the living). In the text it is usually rendered as "unplanned, fortuitous development."

6) Two important hermeneutical terms are *Selbstverständnis* (self-understanding) and *Vorverständnis* (preunderstanding).

a) "self-understanding" means a person's or group's own interpretation of its motives, norms, and goals.

b) "preunderstanding" is the analogue in the sphere of understanding and interpretation to a priori knowledge in the sphere of cognition. That is, it refers to structures of meaning and intention already operative in our approach to what we interpretively understand, which both make possible our understanding and significantly predetermine it.

7) By this time the "life-world" (*Lebenswelt*) has become an accepted term in English. Derived from Husserl, it refers to the irreducible fabric of meanings of everyday life, in which the meanings of specialized, constructed, or formalized languages are embedded.

8) "Mediatization" (*Mediatisierung*) of the population

refers to the suspension of the latter's substantive decision-making power through its encapsulation in organizations and political parties that predefine its needs with regard to the stability of the political system.

9) "Actionism" (*Aktionismus*) means not activism but the policy of direct political action as a compulsive response to all conflict situations.

10) "Critical" retains the Kantian sense of self-reflective examination of the limits and validity of knowledge.

The preparation of this translation called upon the resources of a number of people, all of whom participated not only in the work but in the desire to have the works of Jürgen Habermas available in English. I am particularly grateful to Paul Breines, Charlotte Riley, and Shierry M. Weber for reading parts of the manuscript, making useful revisions, and discussing the substance of these essays with me at length. Barbara Behrendt was helpful by typing and by providing what is still called "moral support." I should also like to thank Volker Meja, Claus Müller, Claus Offe, and Rusty Simonds for clearing up some difficulties.

Jeremy J. Shapiro

CHAPTER ONE

The University in a Democracy
—Democratization of the University*

> *In the vicinity of Sde Boker in the Negev, Israel's large desert, Ben-Gurion wants to found a university town to serve the exploitation of this desert area. The new town is being planned for ten thousand students and the corresponding number of faculty and is to bring Israeli youth into contact with the development of the desert through the acquisition of the necessary knowledge of the natural sciences and technology. It is intended primarily to develop the trained personnel who will be necessary for future industry in the desert. In particular, the development of such industry will involve enterprises that require much scientific knowledge and little raw material.*

This news item appeared in the *Frankfurter Allgemeine Zeitung* of January 11, 1967. If, without additional knowledge, we read it correctly, a university is to serve as an instrument for the industrial development of an almost inaccessible region. From the very beginning industrial production will be initiated at the level of the most advanced technology. For the future of Israel this is probably a vital project. For us, however, the idea of a university as the starting point for the industrialization of a strip of desert is unusual. Yet the Israeli example is not so out of the way. Our educational institutions also have tasks to fulfill in the system of social labor.

Universities must transmit technically exploitable knowledge. That is, they must meet an industrial society's need for

* This essay was originally a lecture given at the Free University of Berlin in January 1967 at the University Conference.

1

qualified new generations and at the same time be concerned with the expanded reproduction of education itself. In addition, universities must not only transmit technically exploitable knowledge, but also produce it. This includes both information flowing from research into the channels of industrial utilization, armament, and social welfare, and advisory knowledge that enters into strategies of administration, government, and other decision-making powers, such as private enterprises. Thus, through instruction and research the university is immediately connected with functions of the economic process. In addition, however, it assumes at least three further responsibilities.

First, the university has the responsibility of ensuring that its graduates are equipped, no matter how indirectly, with a minimum of qualifications in the area of extrafunctional abilities. In this connection extrafunctional refers to all those attributes and attitudes relevant to the pursuit of a professional career that are not contained per se in professional knowledge and skills. The classified advertisements provide weekly information about the catalog of leadership characteristics and loyalties supposed to be possessed by employees in managerial positions. Analogously, judges are expected to be capable of an institutionally adequate exercise of official authority, and doctors of quick action in situations of uncertainty. Of course, the university certainly does not produce the virtues of these unwritten professional standards, but the pattern of its socialization processes must at least be in harmony with them. When this does not happen, conflicts arise. One need only think, for example, of the protests of Protestant congregations against ministers of the younger generation from the Bultmann school. We can be sure that these ministers are not worse exegetes than their predecessors. In short, the problem is not their functional abilities.

Second, it belongs to the tasks of the university to transmit, interpret, and develop the cultural tradition of the society. The influence of interpretations provided by the social sciences and humanities on the self-understanding of the general public can be seen easily. Today the hermeneutic sciences, no matter how positivistically disciplined in their methods, cannot in studying active traditions completely escape the constraint of either continuously reproducing them, or developing them or critically transforming them. We need only recall the recent discussion among German historians about the origins of World War I. Or imagine how future schoolteachers' picture of German classicism would be altered if for one generation the radical authors published by Suhrkamp Verlag occupied the chairs in modern German literature at the universities.

Third, the university has always fulfilled a task that is not easy to define; today we would say that it forms the political consciousness of its students. For too long, the consciousness that took shape at German universities was apolitical. It was a singular mixture of inwardness, deriving from the culture of humanism, and of loyalty to state authority. This consciousness was less a source of immediate political attitudes, than of a mentality that had significant political consequences. Without planned actions, without the organized study of political science and without political education, without the student body's political mandate in questions of current politics, without student political organizations—indeed under the aegis of an apparently apolitical institution—generations of students were educated in the disciplines of knowledge and simultaneously were educated in a politically effective manner. This process reproduced the mentality of a university-trained professional stratum for which society still intended a relatively uniform status. Transcending differences of faculty and profession, this mentality assured the homogeneity of the university-trained elite to the extent that in some leadership groups academic training even sufficed to preserve continuity through the German defeat in 1945. Nevertheless, at the universities themselves this tradition has not survived fascism. As we know, the academic stratum, shaped by a uniform mentality, has dissolved in connection with long-term structural changes in society. Does this mean, however, that today's universities no longer meet the task of providing political education, or, insofar as they take care of this function in another way, no longer need to meet it?

The example of the desert university planned as a center of industrial development suggests the peculiar idea that research and instruction today have to do only with the production and transmission of technologically exploitable knowledge. Can and should the university today restrict itself to what appears to be the only socially necessary function and at best institutionalize what remains of the traditional cultivation of personality as a separate educational subject divorced from the enterprise of knowledge?[1] I should like to argue against this suggestive illusion and advance the thesis that under no circumstances can the universities dispense with the three tasks I have mentioned that go beyond the production and transmission of technologically exploitable knowledge. In every conceivable case, the enterprise of knowledge at the university level influences the action-orienting self-understanding of students and the public. It cannot define itself with regard to society exclusively in relation to technology, that is, to systems of purposive-rational action. It inevitably relates also to practice, that is, it influences communicative action. Nevertheless it is conceivable that a university rationalized as a factory would exert an influence on cultural self-understanding and on the norms of social actors indirectly and without being conscious of its own role in doing so. If the university were exclusively adapted to the needs of industrial society and had eradicated the remains of beneficent but archaic freedoms, then behind the back of its efficient efforts, it could be just as ideologically effective as the traditional university used to be. It could pay for its unreflected relation to practice by stabilizing implicit professional standards, cultural traditions, and forms of political consciousness, whose power expands in an uncontrolled manner precisely when they are not chosen but result instead from the ongoing character of existing institutions.

After 1945 the primary aim of university education in West Germany was to use the dimension of general education, mediated by neohumanism and strongly anchored in institutions, with the goal of educating the citizens of the university to become reliable citizens of the new democratic order. The general-education programs that appeared everywhere were easily connected with political education. The administrators of culture were not petty in establishing chairs in political science and sociology. Student governments were occupied with current political issues and student political organizations were welcomed and promoted. Whether it was interpreted as a formal commitment to political education or not, the political enlightenment of students seemed desirable, especially in the period of the Cold War. If I may generalize, at that time the university was inserted into democratic society with a certain political extension of its traditional self-understanding, *but otherwise just as it was*. Unchanged was the university's crisis-proof foundation of self-governing autonomy. A by-product of the latter, of course, was a certain immobilism, for it turned out to be an impediment to self-motivated university reform. That is why today, two decades after the first post-war reform program, a discontented society has presented the cumbersome university corporation with a bill for which it is admittedly not solely responsible.

In this situation *those* professors who would like to preserve the traditions of the German university are confronted with an alternative. They can read the latest recommendations of the Council on Education and Culture (*Wissenschaftsrat*, a government council on long-term changes in the educational system) as a technologically conceived strategy for adaptation and adopt it. Then they would be sacrificing sanctified foundations of tradition, putting up with regulation, and, above all, saving their own position in a university run by full professors. Or they can interpret it, after discounting the bureaucratically pressured reduction of the length of the course of study, in accordance with the so-called progressives. Then they can keep the university open to that dimension that we associate since the days of German Idealism with the concept of self-reflection. But this, it seems to me, would require the price of a transformation of internal structures.

The link between our postwar democracy and the traditional university—a link that seems almost attractive—is coming to an end. Two tendencies are competing with each other. *Either* increasing productivity is the sole basis of a reform that smoothly integrates the depoliticized university into the system of social labor and at the same time inconspicuously cuts its ties to the political, public realm. *Or* the university asserts itself *within* the democratic system. Today, however, this seems possible in only one way: although it has misleading implications, it can be called *democratization of the university*. I should like to substantiate my vote for this second possibility by trying to demonstrate the affinity and inner relation of the enterprise of knowledge on the university level to the democratic form of decision-making.

The argument with which I begin is borrowed from the philosophy of science, since the traditional self-understanding of scientific inquiry that goes back to Hume argues for the existence of a fundamental *separation* of practice from science and for the coordination of science and technology. Hume demonstrated that normative statements cannot be derived from descriptive statements. Hence it seems advisable not to confuse decisions about the choice of norms, that is, about moral or political problems, with problems of the empirical sciences. From theoretical knowledge we can at best, given specific goals, derive rules for instrumental action. Practical knowledge, on the contrary, is a matter of rules of communicative action and these standards cannot be grounded in a scientifically binding manner. This logical separation thus suggests an institutional separation: Politics does not belong at the university except as the object of a science that itself proceeds according to an unpolitical method.

Now the argument propounded by Hume is not false. But I believe that it does *not* imply the strategy for which Hume's positivistic successors have invoked it. We do not need to judge scientific inquiry only under the logical conditions of the theories that it generates. For another picture emerges if we examine not the results of the process of inquiry but its movement. Thus metatheoretical discussions are the medium of scientific progress—I mean methodological discussions of the utility of an analytic framework, the expedience of research strategies, the fruitfulness of hypotheses, the choice of methods of investigation, the interpretation of the results of measurement, and the implicit assumptions of operational definitions not to mention discussions of theoretical foundations of the fruitfulness of different methodological approaches.

Interestingly enough, however, from the logical point of view, discussions of this kind do not follow rules different from those of any critical discussion of practical questions. This sort of *critical* argumentation is distinguished from straight deductions or empirical controls in that it rationalizes attitudes by means of the justification of a choice of standards. True, the relation between attitudes and statements cannot possibly be one of implication. Yet the approval of a procedure or the acceptance of a norm can be supported or weakened by arguments: it can at least be rationally assessed. And this is precisely the task of critical thought, both for metatheoretical and practical decisions.

Of course it makes a difference whether we are discussing standards that, as in science, establish the framework for descriptive statements or standards that are rules of communicative action. But both are cases of the rationalization of a choice in the medium of unconstrained discussion. In very rare cases practical questions are decided in this rational form. But there is one form of political decision-making according to which all decisions are supposed to be made equally dependent on a consensus arrived at in discussion free from domination—the democratic form. Here the principle of public discourse is supposed to eliminate all force other than that of the better argument, and majority decisions are held to be only a substitute for the uncompelled consensus that would finally result if discussion did not always have to be broken off owing to the need for a decision. This principle, that—expressed in the Kantian manner—only reason should have force, links the democratic form of political decision-making with the type of discussion to which the sciences owe their progress. For we must not overlook the element of decision-making in scientific progress.

Here we see evidence of a subterranean unity of theoretical and practical reason. Today we can only formally take note of this unity; we have no philosophy that could explicate its content. In relation to the sciences, philosophy today can no longer claim an institutionally secured position of privilege, but philosophizing retains its universal power in the form of the self-reflection of the sciences themselves. In this dimension, occupied by philosophy, the unity of theoretical and practical reason that does not hold for scientific theories themselves is preserved. Philosophy, having become circumscribed as a specific discipline, can legitimately go beyond the area reserved to it by assuming the role of interpreter between one specialized narrow-mindedness and another. Thus, I consider it philosophical enlightenment when doctors learn from sociological and psychoanalytic studies to appreciate the influence of the family environment in the genesis of psychoses and thereby also learn to reflect on certain biologistic assumptions of the tradition of their discipline. I consider it philosophical enlightenment when sociologists, directed by professional historians, apply some of their general hypotheses to historical material and thereby become aware of the inevitably forced character of their generalizations. They thus learn to reflect on the methodologically suppressed relation of the universal and the individual. I consider it philosophical enlightenment when philosophers learn from recent psycholinguistic investigations of the learning of grammatical rules to comprehend the causal connection of speech and language with external conditions and in this way learn to reflect on the methodological limits to the mere understanding of meaning. These are not examples of interdisciplinary research. Rather, they illustrate a self-reflection of the sciences in which the latter become critically aware of their own presuppositions.

Such immanent philosophizing also confirms its validity with regard to the transposition of scientific results into the life-world. The translation of scientific material into the educational processes of students requires the very form of reflection that once was associated with philosophical consciousness. The developers of new pedagogical methods for curricula in college-oriented schools should go back to the philosophical presuppositions of the different fields of study themselves. Thus, for example, the transmission of basic grammatical structures in a language class at the primary school level, where the bases of several languages are taught simultaneously and comparatively, cannot be meaningfully discussed without confronting the problems of the philosophy of language as they have developed from Humboldt through Saussure to Chomsky. Similarly pedagogical problems of history instruction on the junior high school level lead to the problems connected with the emergence of the historical consciousness that has developed since the end of the seventeenth century with the tradition of the philosophy of history. Equally important is the demand for self-reflection that such pedagogical questions create for the natural sciences and mathematics. It would be easy to show in the cases of other disciplines the crossover points between theory and practice where self-reflection arises: in jurisprudence the practice of the application of laws leads to problems of hermeneutics, and in the social sciences it is the practical need for aid in decisions and planning which has called forth discussions about basic methodological questions.

   All of these examples characterize a dimension in which the sciences practice reflection. In this dimension they critically account to themselves, in forms originally employed by philosophy, both for the most general implications of their presuppositions for ways of viewing the world and for their relation to practice. This dimension must not be closed off. For only in it is it possible to fulfill in a rational fashion those three functions which the university must in some way deal with over and above the production and transmission of technically exploitable knowledge. Only in this dimension can we promote the replacement of traditional professional ethics by a reflected relation of university graduates to their professional practice. Only in it can we bring to consciousness, through reflection, the relation of living generations to active cultural traditions, which otherwise operate dogmatically. Only in it, finally, can we subject to critical discussion both attitudes of political consequence and motives that form the university as a scientific institution and a social organization. Students' participation in research processes essentially includes participation in this self-reflection of the sciences. But if critical discussions of this type occur in the area of comprehensive rationality, in which theoretical and

practical reason are not yet separated by methodological prohibitions that are necessary on another level, then there is a
continuity between *these* discussions and the critical discussion
of practical questions: critical argument serves in the end only
to disclose the commingling of basic methodological assumptions and action-orienting self-understanding. If this is so, then
no matter how much the self-reflection of the sciences and the
rational discussion of political decisions differ and must be care-
fully distinguished, they are still connected by the common
form of critical inquiry.

Therefore, so long as we do not want to arbitrarily put
a halt to rationalization, we do not need to accept the existence
of an opposition between a university aiming at professional
specialization and one aiming at external politicization. For the
same reason, however, we must not be satisfied with a depoliticized university. Current politics must be able to become part
of the internal university community. I say this even though
a National Democratic Club (a right-wing group associated with
neo-Nazism) has been founded at the University of Frankfurt.
And I believe it possible to advocate this thesis because the only
principle by which political discussions at the universities can
be legitimated is the same principle that defines the *democratic
form* of decision-making, namely: rationalizing decisions in such
a way that they can be made dependent on a consensus arrived
at through discussion free from domination.

This is, as noted, a principle. It is binding but not real.
That is why when considering the process of democratic decision-making we must distinguish, at least for analytical purposes,
between (a) the discussion of proposals and justifications and
(b) the demonstration of a decision with appeal to the preceding arguments. With regard to matters other than conflicts
between parts of the corporation about questions of university
politics, the university is not the place for the demonstration of
political decisions.[2] But it is, I believe, an ideally suited place for
the discussion of political issues, if and to the extent that this
discussion is fundamentally governed by the same rules of rationality within which scientific reflection takes place. This

structural connection also renders comprehensible the fact that students make extensive use of their civil and political rights in order to demonstrate their will outside the university as well. Inversely, however, it is then just as understandable that members of the university are expected, in their role as citizens, to make clear the connection between demonstrations and the argumentation that preceded them.

This thesis seems to be supported by my attempt to demonstrate an immanent relation between the enterprise of knowledge at the university and the critical enterprise. But this relation can also be defended pragmatically by the need for political self-protection. In a democracy that is not firmly established, we must expect masked states of emergency that are *not* interpreted and recognized by the authorities as violations of legality. Often in such cases the only thing that works is the mechanism of self-defense, based on solidarity, undertaken by the whole institution under attack. The particular interest then seems to draw strength from beyond its own limits through an acute convergence with the general interest. The Spiegel affair was an example. In rare unity of spirit the entire press took up arms against this violation of the freedom of the press. A violation of wage autonomy would surely set off a no less united protest by the unions. And so, too, if the constitutional norm that guarantees freedom of instruction and research should ever be violated again, the first resistance should come from the universities themselves, with professors and students side by side. An act of self-defense of this sort could no longer be expected from a depoliticized university.

If for this pragmatic reason we not only permit but promote the critical discussion of practical questions at the university, then students naturally have an even greater right to take part in discussions in which the university itself is a political issue. They have a legitimate role in determining local and national policies about the university and higher education. Now for years an active and logically persuasive minority of students has demanded a democratization of the university.[3] The university run by professors, which simulates a community of teachers and students, would be replaced by a corporation in whose administration all three parties would take part with the opportunity of asserting their own interests: students, junior faculty, and professors. Also, the dualism of academic hierarchy and the administration of institutes would be overcome. Again, students and junior faculty, in accordance with their actual functions, would participate in administering the resources of the institutes. These proposals have been subject to misunderstandings, partly because they are based on false models, for example, workers' codetermination in industrial enterprises.

I cannot discuss this further here. But I am of the opinion that we as professors have no reason to abstain from such discussion. If, for example, the present conflict at the Free University—whose open character, contrary to the lament of part of the press, cannot hurt the universities standing or freedom—can still lead to a politically meaningful result, then it might be the following: the formation at the universities of Berlin and the Federal Republic of joint commissions in which professors confer unrestrictedly with instructors and students about all demands regarding university policy, including the most aggravating ones. And the public should be immediately informed of the results.

CHAPTER TWO

Student Protest in the
Federal Republic of Germany*

Until recently we were convinced that students do not play a political role in developed industrialized societies. They played a revolutionary role in nineteenth-century Russia, in China in the twenties and thirties, and in Cuba in the fifties. In 1956, the revolts in Budapest and Warsaw were set off by student protests. Students are of great political significance especially in the developing areas of Southeast Asia, Latin America, and Africa. Governments in Bolivia, Venezuela, Indonesia, and South Vietnam have been overthrown by students. In countries in which revolutionary nationalist groups, usually army officers, have come to power, students exercise a permanent political pressure. In these cases, three conditions for the politicization of student consciousness are generally present:

1. Students can definitely understand themselves as the future elite of the nation, responsible for a large-scale modernization process. Yet their studies are not organized according to well-defined and socially normative models. The adult role anticipated at the university is thus simultaneously politically important and diffuse in content, and is therefore unsuited for supporting a privatized orientation bound to career and advancement.

2. Students are not only preparing for roles that have political significance, the university itself is an agent of social change. It generates both new, technically exploitable knowledge and the consciousness of modernity, with all of its practical consequences. Thus merely belonging to a university

* This essay was originally a lecture given in November 1967 at the invitation of the Goethe House in New York to inform the American public about the protest movement in the Federal Republic of Germany.

provides an impulse toward entering the struggle against the traditionalism of inherited social structures.

3. The structures of the old society, organized according to kinship relations, are the same as those that define the life of the students' families. Thus, there is a singular parallel between the socialization process of the individual student and the overall process of social change. The student, removed from a traditionalist home and initiated into the universalistic roles of a society in the process of modernization, can connect the typical developmental experiences of adolescence with changes in social structure. He can comprehend the epochal process in the framework of his own educational process and conversely link his private destiny with political destiny.

None of these conditions is present in advanced industrial societies. In Europe and the United States the university has narrowly circumscribed functions, namely preparation for qualified career positions, the production of technically exploitable knowledge, and the transmission of a culture which for centuries science and technology have been rooted in rather than uprooting. Moreover, there is no opposition in principle between parental orientations and the norms and values of modern achievement-oriented society that prevail at the university. Sociological considerations of this sort have led to the prediction that students in our countries cannot attain political significance.[1] Seymour Martin Lipset still holds to this thesis:

> A brief comparative look at the situation of the university and educated youth in the emerging and industrially developed societies suggests that student activism cannot take on major proportions in the latter.[2]

Nevertheless, for two or three years we have been witnessing student protests at our universities that definitely surpass in scope and method the proportions that have been customary since the end of the war. How are we to explain this? I should like to investigate this question, taking West Germany as an example.

I shall concentrate on events in Berlin, for, as is well known, the Free University is the Berkeley of West Germany. Yet the activism of the students of Berlin is echoed at the other West German universities. This has become clear since June 2 of this year. The outrage over the death of Benno Ohnesorg, a politically rather undistinguished student, who was shot by a plainclothesman at a demonstration against the Shah of Iran at the Berlin opera, touched every university in West Germany. Nowhere, to be sure, did these conflicts attain the extent and constancy of the student protests in Berlin, which have been going on since the spring of 1965 and whose end is not yet in sight.

An active, generally highly qualified minority of students, predominantly in the social sciences and humanities, is leading the struggle against the majority of professors, of which the conservative elements are particularly concentrated in the faculties of law and medicine. Since in Germany the universities are state institutions vested with the power of self-government, there are no independent administrations against which students could organize. The faculty is the born opponent. In the intra-university conflicts, three points are at issue. Disregarding specific differences, they correspond to the issues designated here by the phrases "free speech," "knowledge factory," and "student power."[3]

First the question of free speech. The so-called political mandate of the local student government has been disputed since the late forties. The student governments and their umbrella organization, the Verband Deutscher Studentenschaften (Association of German Student Bodies), are compulsory associations based on the automatic membership of all registered students. Hence, the argument that these organizations cannot take a position in the name of student bodies on current political issues is formally correct. On the other hand, the students have pointed out that university problems cannot be neatly separated from those of society as a whole.[4] Given the existing authority structures and the actual division of power at the university, the position of strict legality would be an automatic guarantee of failure. Thus, the political mandate has always been practiced and tacitly accepted. But there remained the legal possibility of restricting the liberties actually taken. In the spring of 1965 the Senate Commissioner of Political Education was censured by the Rector for abuse of office because of an invitation to Karl Jaspers to speak on the twentieth anniversary of the German capitulation and liberation from the Nazi regime. Jaspers declined, and the student parliament invited Erich Kuby, the writer and journalist, to speak in his place. Several years before, Kuby had expressed doubt about the state of freedom at the Free University. The Rector used this as an occasion for prohibiting the speech at the Free University, and it had to be given at the Institute of Technology. This was the beginning of a series of *causes célèbres*. The academic authorities saw themselves called upon to repeatedly restrict the scope of the students' political activity. A few examples: despite his formal apology, an instructor's contract was not renewed because of vague public statements discrediting the Rector. An exhibition about Vietnam was prevented on grounds of violation of housing ordinances. For a while, the use of lecture halls for political events of a not strictly academic character was absolutely denied. Finally, the academic senate attempted to make an "undesirable" political group ineligible for scholarships.

Now to the second point: the knowledge factory. The universities of West Germany have been expanded hesitantly, without structural change, and have since the late fifties, on recommendation of the Government Council on Education and Culture, been externally adapted to the rapidly growing number of students by a linear expansion of the faculty. In institutes and clinics, laboratories and libraries, the mass university affords conditions that discourage many students. The traditionally rigidified courses of study are often unclearly defined and examinations are in many cases burdened with requirements that are antiquated and oriented to the mere reproduction of facts. Only after the recommendations for a reorganization of studies put forth by the Council on Education and Culture in 1966 did the faculties subject the organization of instruction to certain cosmetic operations in order to prevent further interventions. But within a fixed budget and an untouched hierarchical order, these efforts had the immediate effect only of creating more regulation of teaching and study as well as an administratively forced curtailment of attendance at the university. Two of the Berlin faculties hurried to introduce a time limit to immatriculation, that is, to forcibly limit the amount of time that could be spent at the university. There is no doubt that the high dropout rate and the extended duration of study are the result not of bad work attitudes or a poor selection of students, but primarily of catastrophic study conditions and an inadequate organization of university instruction. The students were thus rightly outraged. In the summer of 1966 they demonstratively took action against the restrictive application of the recommendations of the Council. This confrontation resulted in the first major sit-in, in which about three thousand students participated, and led to the establishment of joint commissions on the reform of university study, whose efficacy, nevertheless, remained limited.

This leads us to the third point: student power. Despite an extensive rhetoric of reform, the only comprehensive conceptions for universities in a democratically constituted industrial society have been worked out by students. In the early sixties the Verband Deutscher Studentenschaften, and the Sozialistische Deutsche Studentenbund (German Socialist Student Union, SDS) compiled programs for university reform. Both aimed at the democratization of the university.[5] Students experience the university from a sobering perspective—from below. They see how, under the changed conditions of mass education and a large junior faculty, the perpetuated authority structures of the nineteenth century noticeably inhibit creative development and the rational planning of teaching and research. They understand that they are the prime victims of the absence of university reform. This is why they want to obtain the power of joint decision in all self-governing bodies.

At the same time a new university law has been in preparation in Berlin for years, and an outline of it was made available to the House of Representatives during the summer. Thus the background of the political conflicts at the Free University is overshadowed by the question of whether the Berlin model, which ensures students more extensive rights than their counterparts at any other West German university, should be annulled or at least restricted—or whether it should be expanded in favor of the students.

But in the meantime the conflict crossed the boundaries of the intra-university community. The most active groups among the student body are no longer pursuing university reform. Instead they desire the immediate overthrow of social structures. Radical students have become the backbone of an extra-parliamentary opposition that seeks new forms of organization in clubs and informal centers and a social basis wider than the university. Its first goal is the transformation of the precarious four-power status of Berlin and the establishment of an open city. Campaigns against the Springer Company, which today is unpopular not only among students, serve as the means to mobilization. For the first time in the history of the Federal Republic of Germany, students are playing a political role that must be taken seriously. Kurt Sontheimer has correctly observed that

> After June 2, 1967, the student body, not only of Berlin University, but, thanks to them, of the entire Federal Republic has become a factor in German domestic politics. The parties in the Bundestag (West German Parliament) suddenly rushed into discussions with the leaders of student organizations. Both Kiesinger and Willy Brandt went out of their way to talk to students. . . . It is true that the process of the politicization of academic youth started with university problems, but in the meantime it has long transcended this framework. That is why it cannot be held back by a reform of the university even if the lethargy of that institution allowed for a really fundamental one.[6]

This is the new situation that has become evident only in the last few months. In order to understand it we have to consider two subjects.

Since the beginning of 1966 the intra-university conflict has been enmeshed with a conflict between the politicized sections of the student body and the population and Senate of the city of Berlin. In particular, Vietnam protests have made this conflict break out into the open. While the academic administration reacted with refusals of permission to use university buildings and grounds, budgetary cutbacks, and disciplinary procedures, the measures taken by the Senate of the city of Berlin were less feeble and more questionable. All organs of the government, the police, administration of justice, house of representatives, and the mayor himself distinguished and compromised themselves by foolish prejudice and repression: illegal prohibitions of demonstrations, dubious confiscations and problematic arrests, indefensible court proceedings, open police terror, and a Mayor who even thanked the police after Ohnesorg was shot. A week later more than twelve thousand Berlin students marched behind the coffin of their fellow student.

For more than two decades a smaller group of committed students had engaged in a conventional form of university politics, but without success. Rarely did more than one-third of the student body participate in elections to the student government. In contrast, more than two-thirds of the students took part in an election in May of this year. Now it could be seen how easily they take action as soon as provoked executive bodies and irritated professors respond with administrative force or harassed authority. A harmless example is the reviews of lectures published individually and, moreover, anonymously, in the student newspaper of the Free University. They were made a political affair only by the professors concerned, who gave battle with all the narcissism peculiar to our profession, whether through unspeakable pamphlets or the official power of the Rector. Only with these reactions did assertions about the authoritarian structure of our university gain credibility in the eyes of the mass of students. This mechanism explains the success of the tactics borrowed from the United States of infringing rules and of civil disobedience both inside and outside the university. As in the United States universities are among the most vulnerable institutions. They can be put out of commission relatively easily through provocationism. The most active students take advantage of this.[7] They now seem to regard the campus as nothing but a training ground for the mobilization of troops. Their target is no longer the university as such, which has become too inconsiderable an opponent.

In order to explain this situation, which sociologists are not the only ones to have failed to anticipate, I should like to turn to some circumstances that have resulted from both intra-university and general political developments since the war. First I should like to mention some factors specific to Berlin.

The Free University differs from other West German universities in three ways. First, a liberal university constitution accords the student body extensive rights and powers. These also provide the tactical advantage of a basis of legitimation for claims that go beyond the status quo. Second, the composition of the student body, as shown by empirical studies, favors politicization owing to selective immigration from West Germany. In addition, the influx of students from the German Democratic Republic, which stabilized a basic anti-Communist attitude, has ceased since the building of the wall separating the halves of the city. In the academic year 1956–57, almost one-third of the students were from the East; in 1964–65, their proportion had sunk to about 5 percent. Third, the proportion of politically conscious and liberal-minded professors at some of the Berlin faculties is, in my estimation, considerably higher than at universities in the Federal Republic. Hence, students in Berlin have always been able to count on the solidarity of a group of their professors.

On the other hand, the population and government of Berlin were benevolently satisfied with students voicing political positions as long as they kept within the bounds of conformity to prevalent views. From 1958 on, after a student congress opposing the atomic armament of the West German army, conflicts multiplied. For in Berlin, the Cold-War syndrome has been preserved more strongly than in the Federal Republic. Three facts are relevant. First, the Berlin press is monopolized by the anti-intellectual and *ressentiment*-filled newspapers of the Springer Company. Second, owing to the special strategic situation of the city, the Berlin police are trained as a militia in case of civil war. It is unprepared for the political role of noncon-forming minorities. Finally, the government watches nervously over the susceptible organism of a city that is not only politically dependent but also economically endangered by shrinking in-dustrial production and a population heavily overbalanced in the older age-group.

However, these circumstances specific to Berlin cannot fully explain the conflicts that for years have crystallized around issues and events that yield effective publicity. At most they explain the intensification and explosive outbreak of conflicts that have also begun at West German universities in general. But if Berlin is only a model case, what are the causes of the politicization of the consciousness of our students?

Student discontent has causes inside and outside the university. Within the university the malaise has been growing for two decades, because the universities cannot stir themselves to undertake an overdue root-and-branch reform. The German university emerged from the defeat of the Nazi regime with increased autonomy in self-government. But the cost of the immunity granted by guild privileges is immobility. Therefore, the process of integrating the old university into a modern in-dustrial society has been taking place without will and con-sciousness. This unplanned structural change in our university can be comprehended sociologically from two points of view.[8] First, Humboldt's university, which dominated the nineteenth century, was an elite institution from which broad strata were excluded—not even the petit bourgeoisie was admitted, in con-trast to the United States. Second, the educational process was not, as, for example, in Great Britain, oriented to defined profes-sional and social models. The educational process of the uni-versity of scholars was reserved for the few and was predomi-nantly oriented to the requirements of research. The university was supposed to educate and cultivate, but it did not train masses or experts. Since then both functions have become inevitable—even though admission to German universities is still largely determined by privilege (for ten years the proportion of chil-dren of workers has fluctuated around 5 to 6 percent), even though many courses of study still appear as though they were to serve the creation of a younger generation of great scholars rather than preparation for a professional career. Measured against the objective needs of society, the university system does not function effectively. The number of those who actually obtain degrees is too low, the length of study too long, the qualifications acquired are often inadequate, and research is stagnating in many areas. That is why political pressure from without has increased within recent years. The press, representatives of political parties, the bureaus of education, and economic interest groups are all pushing energetically for measures of rationalization in the large-scale bureaucratic organization that the university is today. Professors of the old style, in contrast, have their backs to the wall and are attempting to assert positions that are almost of merely rhetorical value. The more active part of the student body, and some of their teachers who are considered liberal, see the danger of a compromise between the two camps. They fear that the professors will sacrifice sacred foundations of tradition, put up with regulation, and in exchange maintain the inviolability of their own position. They will, the students fear, accept as the goal of reform an augmentation of efficiency that will without friction integrate a depoliticized university into the system of social labor, *and* at the same time, save the predominant position of professors in the university. These students want neither the traditional university, elitist and classically humanistic, nor the mass university as a mere school for experts—nor, above all, a combination of the worst elements of both.

The causes outside the university are not as easy to reduce to a common denominator. In the first postwar period, until about the mid-fifties, student protest was defined by clear issues: the danger of Communism, a united Europe, rearmament, and the Nazi past. Only two of these protest movements that shaped the political climate at the universities during the first half of the fifties are important for understanding the present situation. The first, directed against the rearmament of the Federal government, was associated with ideas of a neutralist foreign policy and with fear of the socially restorative ramifications of a reestablished *Wehrmacht* (Army). This protest was part of a general opposition which at the time was still led by the Social-Democratic Party. The second movement was centered mainly at the universities, but still was embedded in a more wide-ranging opposition: the protest against the veiled continuity of the present with the heritage of the Nazi period. This pre-dominantly morally based protest against the absence at almost all levels of a radical confrontation with the traditions of the recent past was expressed, for example, in a wave of demonstra-tions against films of Veit Harlan, the Nazi movie director and actor, or in the successful resistance of students and professors at the University of Göttingen to the appointment of Schlüter, a former Nazi, as Minister of Education in Lower Saxony. Both protest movements were soon without object. By the mid-fifties rearmament already had been decided upon as had the long-term establishment of a regime that accepted Globke and Seebohm as honorable men. It is true that the old opposition flamed up again in 1957–58 when the atomic armament of the federal army was debated, and that trials of Nazis have been initiated in the past few years. But the left opposition, for whose chain of frustrations the Frankfurt Paulskirche has become a symbol, finally had to capitulate to the victorious course of the Christian Democratic Union. The Social-Democratic Party drew the relevant conclusions at the end of the fifties. It gradually aban-doned the role of opposition party and followed the strategy of participating in the existing government rather than replacing it.

Three tendencies, I believe, have determined, in increas-ing measure, the situation of the remaining intellectual opposi-tion in our country during the last decade. These tendencies make clear why the oppositional sectors of today's student body are no longer content with this situation. First, the intellectual opposition has been increasingly isolated and has lost its connec-tion with political organizations especially with the political parties. SDS, the strongest political student group, was excluded from the Social-Democratic Party, while associations of literati, such as Gruppe 47 (Group 47), have engaged themselves in-creasingly in questions of current politics. Second, it has in-creasingly abandoned setting forth alternatives and limited itself to resignedly affirming the remains of liberalism. These defensive means accord with the diffuse opponent and the conservative goal. The *Spiegel* affair is the model case of defensive mobilization of the public in the name of violated constitutional rights. Third, representatives of the intellectual opposition have gotten ahead in the artistic and literary world, radio and television organizations, and universities and research institutes. In their way they have become part of the establishment. And the prohibition of the Communist party does its part in restricting the scope of the legitimated use of language. That is, it purges the opposition's language and thought of components of left-wing traditions that have been made illegal.

The annual Easter march of the German Campaign for Nuclear Disarmament, which is celebrated in the consciousness of its own fruitlessness, is today the only recognized ritual of mass protest. It characterizes the situation to which our students are now responding. The wave of protest that was released starting on June 2 has removed the veil from new forms of reaction. We of an older generation reacted to this event, which Günter Grass has called the first political murder of the Federal Republic of Germany, the way we reacted to the night-and-fog action against the *Spiegel:* as an additional symptom of the restriction of democratic rights and an alarm signal for a renewed defensive attempt. But for the active part of the student body, June 2 means something different.

These students belong to the first generation whose memory is not determined by the Nazi period and its immediate consequences: the first generation that knows no economic insecurity and relative poverty: the first generation that did not witness the emergence of the institutional framework of the Federal Republic but instead is acquainted with the mass democracy of the welfare state and with organized capitalism simply as the established order. These students therefore have no personal experience of political terror, economic crises, real political alternatives to the established order, and of organized opposition. Moreover, they belong to the first generation that openly perceives the disproportion between the potential wealth and potential gratification of an industrially developed society, and the actual life of the masses in that society. They are the first generation that no longer understands why, despite the high level of technological development, the life of the individual is still determined by the ethic of competition, the pressure of status-seeking, and the values of possessive individualism and socially dispensed substitute-gratifications. They do not understand why the institutionalized struggle for existence, the discipline of alienated labor, or the eradication of sensuality and aesthetic gratification should be perpetuated—why, in short, the mode of life of an economy of poverty is preserved under conditions of a possible economy of abundance. On the basis of a *fundamental* lack of sympathy with the senseless reproduction of now superfluous virtues and sacrifices, the rising generation has developed a particular sensitivity to the untruth of prevailing legitimations. Outrage against the double standards of the older generation's morality is, of course, repeated in every generation. But today protest is directed against a society that has lent the emancipatory ideals of the eighteenth century the force of constitutional norms and has accumulated the potential for their realization—while it has not abolished hunger in the world of potential abundance, while it has widened the gap between industrial and developing nations, exporting misery and military violence along with mass hygiene. This is the symbolic meaning that American intervention in the Vietnamese civil war has taken on today in the eyes not only of many American students but of most German students as well.

Against this background it is easier to understand what is really new about the most recent protest movements, namely what one could call the "neoanarchist worldview" and the predilection for direct action. In what follows I shall be speaking of a relatively small, very active minority whose attitude is, if I am not mistaken, symptomatic of a trend.

The worldview of these students is shaped by the impression that social institutions have coalesced into a relatively closed, conflict-free and self-regulating, yet violent, apparatus. Enlightenment and opposition can be provided only by uncorrupted individuals on the margins of the apparatus. Whoever assumes a function within it, however unimportant, becomes integrated and neutralized. Thus there are no defined opponents within society; there are no allies and no designatable social groups as agents of protest. In these circumstances protest itself must assume the form of provocation, of going beyond the legitimate rules of the game. Its goal is immediate mobilization of many individuals for the sake of mobilization itself. This recalls certain political doctrines that Sorel derived from the basic assumptions of Bergson's vitalism. I myself at first considered this a plausible historical connection. Today I am no longer certain how far the parallel extends. The new actionism and the worldview of the new anarchism borrow from Mao and Castro, although the field of operations is defined by our large cities and not at all by the conditions of underdeveloped agrarian nations. The new tactics have the advantage of obtaining rapid publicity. But they also bear dangers, which students themselves have observed: the danger of diversion either into the privatization of an easily consolable hippie subculture or into the fruitless violent acts of the actionists.

In attempting to explain this more extensive political commitment we come upon factors that are not specific to developments in the Federal Republic of Germany alone. It could be that our students are reacting to a specific situation but that they are impelled by motives that could generally take form for the first time during the fifties under the conditions of life of the industrially most advanced societies. A rough comparison of student protest in the Federal Republic and in the United States supports this conjecture.

In the Federal Republic and in the United States the immediate frustrations and burdens of study cannot have the same causes. In the United States, especially at the college level, there is the noticeable pressure of a planned organization of instruction with standardized norms of achievement and its frequent testing. In comparison, instruction at the philosophical faculties of German universities, the centers of the disturbances, is diffuse and inadequately organized. German students are only anticipating the specific necessities of a socially adapted training of experts that are already in effect in the United States.

The political contexts outside the universities are also

quite different. In the United States the underprivilege of the black population, and the war in Vietnam are two acute, clearly defined and obvious conflicts, which daily produce new violence and therefore provoke counterviolence. In Germany manifest conditions of a comparable order of magnitude are lacking. Naturally in the Federal Republic there are the permanent conflicts of organized welfare-state capitalism and the particular conflicts of a divided nation. But we have no ghettos that could possibly serve as the basis for urban guerrilla actions, and no students who are drafted to fight guerrillas in Southeast Asia. In the Federal Republic conflicts smoulder under the cover of an integrated society having a slighter measure of open aggressiveness. The attempts of our activists to challenge and make manifest the violence of institutions are therefore a bit superficial compared with the actions of the New Left in the United States. Aside from temporary technological unemployment in the mining industry in the Ruhr, the only conflict outside the universities that obtrudes itself and does not have to be staged is opposition to the planned emergency laws. Here the opposition is led by a coalition of trade unionists and intellectuals, and not primarily by rebellious students.

Finally, what is most lacking in the background of the New Left in Germany is the hippie scene. So far, drugs do not appear to be in use at German universities to any extent worth mentioning. Other sedatives, too—I mean orientations that channel outwardly directed protest into apolitical paths, such as yoga and Zen Buddhism—have not yet gained any recognizable influence. The potential discontent that is obviously growing among students can therefore take political form to a greater extent than appears to be the case in the United States. In addition, there is in Europe, in contradistinction to America, an almost unbroken theoretical tradition influenced by Hegel and Marx. This may explain why new student attitudes are articulated more rapidly in West Germany.

Despite these differences the student protests in the two countries resemble each other. Through its mere extent and degree of intransigence the protest distinguishes the new student movement from previous, conventional oppositional currents. In both countries we observe the provocationist tactics that intentionally violate liberal rules, refrain from coalitions with groups inside the system, and would like to keep open a zone of unalienated existence on the margins of the system. In both countries we observe the fundamental attitudes that find expression in the features of a neoanarchist worldview whether emotionally on the level of the Beatles and folk songs, politically on the level of Castroism and quotations from Chairman Mao, or reflectively on the level of a theory that somewhat existentializes Marx and Freud, as in the works of Herbert Marcuse. But if structural developments within the university and the political situation outside it do not reveal enough common features to make plausible the correspondence of the protest actions that we can observe in the two countries, then, we must look for the important causes on another, deeper level.

Participants in student protests are almost exclusively bourgeois youth—"white middle class kids"—who do not represent the working class, or blacks, or the underdeveloped countries but want to act for them and in their name. If my observations are correct, these students do not understand themselves as intellectuals who renounce their social class and place themselves as an avant-garde at the head of the oppressed and exploited. They set no store by the rights institutionalized in bourgeois constitutions, for they do not doubt that the established system could eventually integrate even those groups not yet integrated today—this is, in fact, precisely what they fear. The achievements of the past appear to these students as models of integration, which have absorbed only too effectively all oppositional forces. So we are confronted here with the first bourgeois revolt against the principles of a bourgeois society that is almost successfully functioning according to its own standards. What is in question is not the system's productivity and efficiency but rather the way in which the system's achievements have taken on their own life and become independent of the needs of the people who live in it.

The protest of youth from bourgeois homes no longer seems primarily a protest against parental authority, as was the case for generations. This generation has probably grown up with more psychological understanding, a more liberal education, and under the influence of more permissive attitudes than all previous generations. American studies show in addition that active members of left-wing student groups frequently have parents who share and encourage their critical attitude. Comparable data are lacking for the Federal Republic. I suspect that the bourgeois-authority syndrome has more importance; but tendencies similar to those in the United States are visible in West Germany. If we also take into account the fact that this generation is the first to have grown up under less burdensome economic conditions, and is therefore psychologically less subject to the disciplinary compulsion of the labor market, then we can hypothesize a context on the basis of which we can explain the singular sensitivity of young activists: They have become sensitive to the costs for individual development of a society dominated by competition for status and achievement and by the bureaucratization of all regions of life. These costs seem to them disproportionately high in relation to the technological potential. The young have become very sensitive to the dangers of an order that does not avert aggression but increases it militarily and economically—that produces strategic risks on a planetary scale and creates the modern pauperism of the Third World.

We sociologists did not reckon with the possibility that students could play a political role in developed industrial societies. The values of status-mobile and socially climbing middle-class families accord with the universalistic values of the university tradition. And no drastic upheaval of political structures is forseeable that could find a parallel in educational processes and the experiences of adolescents. Or is this assumption perhaps incorrect? I have mentioned three conditions for the politicization of the consciousness of students that are fulfilled in typical developing nations. The third condition was a certain parallel between processes of personal development and revolutions of social structure (that is, between dissociation from the traditionalist home and the dissolution of traditionalist social formations). This parallelism favors the association of private and political destiny. I wonder whether an analogous condition is not fulfilled in those industrially developed societies that have already crossed the threshold to potential abundance.

It could very well be that the dissolution of parental authority and the spreading of permissive educational techniques make possible experiences and promote orientations among children that necessarily conflict with the standards of the perpetuated ideology of achievement while simultaneously converging with technologically available, although socially enchained, potential leisure and freedom, gratification and pacification. It could very well be that industrial society in the United States and Europe has attained a level of development at which the problems of structural social change, as at the transition to modernization, *once again* find in the formative processes of the rising generations a correspondence with psychological development.

If student protest is more than the expression of a fashion of the present generation, then we should not lose sight of this question. Perhaps the process of petrification of our administered consciousness has progressed so far that insensitivity to what in more naive times philosophers called "the good life" can only be broken through today under the sociopsychologically exceptional conditions of university study.

CHAPTER THREE

The Movement in Germany:
A Critical Analysis*

While the government and political parties put forward
hesitant, mainly technocratic reform policies and calls for law
and order, the population's sentiments against students are
growing. Thus the definitions of revolution upheld by left and
right, while equally fictions, can mutually confirm each other.
The left's misleading total perspective and the right's affirma-
tion of the status quo without any perspective could mesh,
bringing about through the method of self-fulfilling prophecy
what has always been evoked: the application of naked repression. The protest movement must not let itself be drawn into
the foreseeable defeat of its actionistic blunders. On the other
hand, conservatives should not misjudge the results of a certainly feasible, short-term, repressive pacification of the universities. In order to avoid both, a sober analysis is needed of
what the protest movement is and can do—and what it is not
and cannot do. The empirical bases for such explanations are
unsystematic and weak. The interpretation that I propose also
can claim no more than a certain plausibility.

Three Intentions

If one keeps to what the most active groups express
and how they behave, three intentions become visible.
The slogan of the Great Refusal denotes a widespread

* In the winter of 1968–69 violent political actions at German
universities, especially at Frankfurt, reached their climax. Student protest
seemed close to a dead end. At that time I attempted to confront the
students' illusory self-evaluation with an unsparing diagnosis. Since then
my fears have unfortunately been proved justified. In March 1970 in
Frankfurt the SDS formally disbanded.

attitude, which mirrors the experience of the ineffectiveness of political opposition in the Western mass democracies. This experience of the absorption of contradiction is the starting point of the resistance. It wants to keep from being integrated and to ensure that the all-pervasive system of mass media will recoil from it and not be able to use it as an alibi for illusory liberality. The new techniques of protest are directed at any phenomenon at random, because any one is appropriate for expressing rejection of an abstractly conceived totality that, it would seem, can only be denounced from outside. Demonstrations have taken the form of obvious provocations that produce immediately consumable offenses or counter-aggressions. The singular character of self-satisfaction which protest thereby obtains, renders it independent of criteria of the success of purposive-rational action. These factors unite in the striving to create counter-worlds, which are supposed to protect against the danger of integration and to convert protest into a way of life that absolves those who lead it of having to ascertain the effectiveness of protest. Every calculated realization of interests, whether of preserving or changing the system, is ridiculed.

The devaluation of the political sphere as an area of purposive-rational action is connected with another intention. The anti-authoritarian attitude rejects the imperatives of achievement. Its objection is not really to specific personality traits and types of personal dependence but to the objectified compulsions of, as it is called, an authoritarian achieving society. This, too, is based on experience. For the sorts of discipline still imposed on the individual in industrially advanced societies no longer have in their favor the outward appearances of an economy of poverty. They must instead assert themselves against the evidence of surplus and potential wealth, especially in the parental homes of our most activist students. Since, in the prototypical area of sexuality, bourgeois virtues have quietly begun to disintegrate as a system of now superfluous sacrifices and dysfunctional repressions, the values of possessive individualism have fallen under general suspicion as historically obsolete and therefore repressive. The ethics of competitive achievement and the dictates of career orientation—indeed all motivations of a society based on status competition—become especially dubious in a social environment in which the young grow up far from the sphere of production and encounter reality only through the filter of consumer orientations and mass media.

In comparison to the forms of bureaucratic domination the model of decision-making through democratic councils seems increasingly convincing, the more that justifications for existing norms are associated in a confusing manner with traditionally exercised status privileges that are kept out of discussion. Functional imperatives are interlocked with inherited domination: the organization of instruction and research at universities provides sufficient examples. This fusion is the soil in which the concept of technocracy—and hatred of it—grows and confirms itself. Mistrust of technocratic developments, which justify norms of domination through reference to so-called objective exigencies, is warranted. But it gets mixed with exaggerated generalizations that can turn into sentiment directed against science and technology as such. Precisely among student activists, there are a number who respond to their psychically induced learning blocks with an almost compulsive rejection of requirements of competence and achievement orientations. From this they sometimes go over into explicit hostility to theory.

This devaluation of theory and the overhasty subordination of theoretical work to the *ad hoc* requisites of practice are connected with a third intention. The slogan of the New Immediacy designates an attitude that radically rejects adaptation to self-regulating systems in favor of immediate gratification. This is based on the experience that complex detours through systems of purposive-rational action continually postpone goals. Today motives of action are increasingly linked to generalized means for attaining random goals, and are exhausted in abstract endeavors to acquire income, leisure time, prestige, influence, etc.—and all this beneath the crust of a specific boredom. It is to this that a number of students are reacting with the insistence that aesthetic experience, instinctual gratification, and expression be realized here and now.

The life-style of protest is defined by sensuous and

sensual qualities. The characteristics of hippie culture have been immediately set loose from their places of origin and widely diffused—and they are not mere decoration. The core of the protest movement—especially in America and England, but in West Germany as well—consists of subcultures whose aim is to overcome the atomization of the state of private learning through experiences of group solidarity. In this way categories of fraternal relations receive a new significance. At the same time, the bourgeois educational process, which has directed the young to individuation by means of the solitary reading of the printed word, is retiring into the background. Experiments with forms of "unalienated" group life generated by youth naturally not only create sensitivity to atrophied modes of experiencing interaction, but also give rise to new conflicts. Their obverse consists of actions that can scarcely be considered as still within a political context. In fact, they serve the immediate instinctual gratification of their initiators—mainly the simple release of aggression.

This summary description of the movement's three intentions can only delimit a potential that no one expected and that still cannot be satisfactorily explained. The basic orientations mentioned do not coincide with the interpretations that define the self-understanding of the protest groups. These justifications rest loosely on the attitudes in which they are rooted. I would not exclude the possibility that coming generations will reject the interpretations prevailing today as soon as the protest potential is displaced to unpolitical areas. (There are signs of this.) I should like to distinguish three justifications. The first comes from Marxism, the second from anarchist traditions, the third from aspects of the cultural revolution.

First Justification: The Theory of Imperialism

Primarily a single complex from the Marxist tradition has become important for the rebels' self-understanding: the theory of imperialism. The domestic use of Marxist slogans (and that is all that they are) would not even be credible on the national scene if the liberation movements of the Third

World had not given the theory of imperialism a new impetus. The Vietnam war has made students aware of the political and economic aspects of the process of decolonization. The struggle for political liberation in the former colonial areas is at the same time a struggle for social liberation. Its declared goal is the elimination of external economic dependence and an internal structure that impedes industrial development. But the theory of imperialism, developed for a past phase of exploitation, no longer adequately explains the growing disparities in the development of rich and poor nations today. The underprivileged state of the developing nations will in the future be increasingly less comprehensible through the category of exploitation needed by the developed systems. But all signs point to the fact that the industrially developed societies—in the sphere of bureaucratized state socialism, no less than in that of organized capitalism—are unable to generate motivations adequate to providing effective aid for economic development oriented to the interests of the recipient nations. A hunger catastrophe surpassing all known dimensions is foreseeable. Even if the theory of imperialism no longer offers adequate explanations, it still indicates quite exactly the phenomenon that needs to be explained: that the established social systems are incapable of solving the problems of survival in other parts of the world. An international situation of class struggle would reemerge if China succeeded in creating an adequate industrial potential for atomic threats without at the same time developing the form of bureaucratic domination and the mentality that hitherto has always accompanied a society's industrialization.

However, militant students use the theory of imperialism to insert their own protest into a false global framework. They feign a world-historical unity of resistance to capitalism, which is supposed to extend from guerrilla struggles in South America and Asia, through black revolts in North American cities and the Chinese Cultural Revolution, to resistance in the "metropolises." In this context the clear differences between the motivations and goals of student revolts in rich and poor, or capitalist and socialist, nations disappear. The correspondence of slogans and techniques, which can be explained by diffusion, obscures the fact that student revolts in these different areas have practically nothing to do with each other.

Second Justification: Neoanarchism

To the new anarchism, the institutional system of developed industrial societies appears as an almost static, or at least well-integrated whole, within which each element, to the extent that it fulfills any function at all, necessarily serves the maintenance of the system. Those who adopt this perspective must look for potential forces of social change beneath the level of the "apparatus." This leads to two unorthodox conclusions. The "base," the only possible source of change, is no longer the process of production but rather the immediate individuals themselves, who are subjected to the compulsive behavioral norms of large organizations. In addition, there are no key groups whose position in the productive process would mark them out for possible enlightenment: revolutionary consciousness can be awakened all along the margins of the system.

The rational core of the new anarchism is the understanding that the latency of class conflict alters the zones of conflict.[1] The struggle for a share of social rewards leads to conflict only in those areas which are not sufficiently protected from disparities in development (and consequent relative deprivation) by organized political pressure. But such conflicts cannot fundamentally endanger the system. In contrast, what cannot be overlooked are conflicts that cannot be peacefully resolved within the governmentally regulated market and distributive sphere through such social rewards as income, leisure time, and social security. These conflicts are set off by needs that do not fall within the reach of the welfare-state administration, needs bearing primarily on the social prerequisites of humane social and community life. Social welfare expenditures (such as education, health, transportation, housing, leisure, etc.) are neglected because, in relation to the sphere of private economic activity, the public-service sector in the institutional framework of advanced capitalism is not expanded to the extent necessary today. Secondly, these needs bear on the possibility of decision-making about the forms, goals, and content of humane social and community life. This need for self-determination is also structurally neglected, because the weak legitimation of advanced capitalism is compensated for by a depoliticized public realm. Both categories of needs arise in the experience of interaction. This, therefore, is where conflicts arise that cannot be solved in authoritarian welfare states. They are not immediately political but have instead a psychological character.

This consideration supports the assumption that the political system can no longer be disturbed by directed attacks in the framework of organized group conflicts, but only by the demoralization of many individuals with regard to their willingness to comply. This requires potential discontent arising from psychically induced conflicts, which cannot be eliminated by means of material rewards. What makes possible the dissolution of the petit-bourgeois need structure is not material poverty, but economic release from status-oriented, acquisitive striving. Yet this hypothesis, which is the only possible ground for neo-anarchist expectations, at the same time drastically restricts these expectations. The need structure that took shape over centuries under the competitive pressure of a market economy was transferred long ago to an integrated labor force. If only a post-scarcity psychology engenders sensitivity to the administered forms of life and labor in which social wealth has been accumulated historically, if only, to put it bluntly, the experience of being glutted with attainable prosperity awakens sensitivity to the neglected area of practical problems of the "good life" (which today are no longer decided in advance by tradition), then revolution in the most developed societies would not bring about the abolition of poverty but presuppose it. In the meantime, discontent that is immune to what the welfare state can offer in the way of compensation could only arise in small privileged groups. Even during the Paris May revolt the resistance of the working class, which resulted from conventional failures of capitalist planning, was not really at one with the student uprising. The two sides obviously had different motivations. In these circumstances, revolutionary claims, even when altered to mean the diffuse, permanent-revolutionary learning process of a growing number of psychologically insecure individuals, are only empty phrases. The rhetoric of revolution lends itself too easily to projections that prevent the real causes of the protest movement from being clarified.

Third Justification: Cultural Revolution

"Cultural revolution" is the catchword for the factors belonging to the third interpretation. It reclaims revolutionary urgency for the many imprecise efforts directed toward the "abolition of culture," although a time-worn modernism has long robbed the "abolition" model of its credibility. The mobilization of youth in China came to an end on order from above. It is hard to say what this Far Eastern Cultural Revolution really means. To account for its stimulation of our own Mao buttons and Red Books we need to conjecture no more than that the Chinese Cultural Revolution served to reawaken in the younger generation consciousness of the original revolutionary situation. Be that as it may, student protest in any case suggests interpretation in terms of cultural revolution—for the participants, because the primary experiences of students are of cultural products and institutions, and for the observer, because the protest movement so far has had results exclusively in the sphere of the "superstructure."

Those who proclaim the end of art—whether artists themselves, literati, or middlemen of the culture industry—and now make up the chorus for a revolution that makes its entrance as illusion are impelled by the experience of resignation. The verbose death notices are motivated not by hope for the realization of symbolic meaning and expression, but by doubt of the credibility of aesthetic means. The more radical among them assert that the artist must lay down his paintbrush or pen because the categories of beauty have gone over from the world of aesthetic allusion to that of political action. The more liberal, who know that after the declarations are completed they will return to their studio or desk, leave open some loopholes: one may abandon art, but only at one's own risk. Finally, the more conventional believe that the cultural revolution is given its due by reducing art to agitation: reportage replaces belles-lettres. Analogous declarations, though more poorly formulated, are made at the universities. Here the goal is the abolition of knowledge: while art, at least, is only ideology, knowledge is direct repression. The New Knowledge will emerge spontaneously, as it were, from political practice, the immemorial stream of life.

However, even art that has become political protest only expands the art market and the stocks of museums. Allegedly moribund art is awakened from the dead by commercialization, which then provides reinforcement for its mummification in museums. More logical than the grand gesture of dismissing culture is, therefore, the intentional fusion of art and consumers' goods. Pop Art precipitates objects out of their functional contexts: as artificial rubbish, the trivial components of a technical civilization gain sensuous quality and unexpected prominence. This is still critique even if at its lowest level. An affirmative culture that undercuts it only arises when liquidated art serves immediately to promote the circulation of commodities—when it mobilizes the devouring of clothes and furniture and bric-a-brac to the point where the borrowed identities of instant and permanent consumers dissolve. This bad utopia of immediacy is based on a psychology of regression that is also to be found among militant students: when culture returns to being second nature, ego structures too are liquidated.

The abolitionist slogans of the cultural revolution may succeed in smashing up pianos and removing the inhibition of aggressive fantasies. But the linguistic system of art only changes immanently, and in such a way that the intentions of the old language can enter into the new one. The active assault upon culture is based on the same reification as the fetishism of those students who believe that by occupying university classrooms they are taking possession of science as a productive force. I consider dangerous the illusion that it is not just *particular* traditions which must repeatedly be shattered, but the continuity of history as such—that it is not just epochal relations of subjects to the symbolic systems of their world- and self-interpretation which must *repeatedly* be abandoned, but symbolic mediation as such. Whoever adheres to these illusions propagates irrationalism.

Today the abstract abolition of culture would only mean that subjectively unleashed beliefs and expressions are removed from the possibility of being translated into revolutionized linguistic systems that are once again capable of being communicated. They would be removed from the possibility of being critically appropriated and turned into demonic powers.

The Actual Results

The three interpretations that determine the self-understanding of the protest movement in its militant form have rational elements. But as a whole they coincide so little with empirically supported judgments of reality that some of their contents have become *idées fixes*. Especially among actionist groups, syndromes of this sort have already been terminologically rigidified. The protest movement has decisively altered the political consciousness of students in West German universities. Existing studies allow the conclusion that students have been politicized to an unexpectedly great extent, without as yet having been polarized into two camps. Measured against the conventional criteria of political attitudes, the democratic potential at the universities is stronger than at any time since the war. Indeed, empirical indicators speak for the correctness of the assertion that today for the first time since before the Revolution of 1848 a "left" student generation predominates at German universities.

With the aid of provocationism inspired by ample fantasy, the most active student groups have tested the scope of the field of action. Contrary to resigned predictions and restrictive anticipations (including my own), successful advances were made into untrodden zones of legitimations that had become fragile. Spontaneous appeals to prevailing legitimations have generated a pressure for legitimation which is of great consequence at those points where institutions can still be affected by a confrontation of idea and reality. Despite everything, this is the case with the university. After almost two and a half decades chances for reform going beyond rhetoric and adaptive pragmatism have now arisen under the pressure of protest.

Incitements to democratization have immediately influenced both the churches and the cultural world. Reform efforts in the administration of justice and the press are more indirect results. These impulses seem to have extended even to the codetermination policy of the unions, and at places to the inner structure of the political parties with regard to questions of educational policy. Looking beyond the short term, remote political effects of student protest could even occur precisely where the actionists neither expect nor want them: in political parties, unions, and mass organizations.

These results of protest, intended and unintended, are ironic. For those who have had success with new demonstration techniques fancy themselves revolutionary fighters against fascist oppression while they are actually doing nothing but polemically exploiting the unexpected latitude granted by liberal institutions. Because militant groups confuse the reality levels of actual power and actions that could corrode the legitimation of power, they unhesitatingly overstep the bounds within which the new forms of demonstration can be efficacious.

That protest has brought to consciousness the distinction between technical and practical problems is, as I see it, a critical achievement. Attacking the ideology of the achieving society has made clear that today citizens' needs are recognized only within certain definitions. In the first place, the only groups in a position to advance their interests with the prospect of success are those whose refusal to participate in collective undertakings has consequences that endanger the system. That is why, in the given political framework, citizens can make their needs felt effectively only to the extent of their participation in system-relevant achievements. In the second place, these needs themselves are always already operationalized in categories of economically and administratively disposable rewards. Publicly tolerated definitions extend to what we need for life (income, leisure time, and security), but not to how we should like to live if we could find out, in view of available potentials, how we could live. The awareness that it is at all possible to discuss such practical questions only emerged in connection with the protest movement. Thus, for example, experiments with new forms of extended families have regained current relevance. Another example is anti-authoritarian kindergartens, although I should not like to conceal my irritation at the experimental carefreeness with which these projects are undertaken, in view of their dubious psychological assumptions.

Finally, I consider the politicization of private conflicts a singular result of the protest movement. The shift to the psychological dimension has altered the medium in which conflicts and discussions of political import are carried out. This is a new fact. Previously, revolutions, and especially pseudo-revolutionary youth movements, have always incorporated motives of deviant behavior, in other words, clinical potential. There is nothing new about the political role of neurotics nor about the introduction by one side in a political struggle of clinical concepts in order to discredit the other. What is characteristic is rather that today the use of psychopathological concepts has become necessary for the identification and explanation of a political state of affairs. Neither the political efficacy of psychic conflicts, nor the psychological reinterpretation of political conflicts, is at the root of the situation's peculiarity. What is peculiar is the short term displacement of the culturally normative border between private and public conflicts. Today, difficulties that a mere two or three years ago would have passed for private matters—for conflicts between students and teachers, workers and employers, or marital partners, for conflicts between individual persons—now claim political significance and ask to be justified in political concepts. Psychology seems to turn into politics—perhaps a reaction to the reality that politics, insofar as it relates to the masses, has long been translated into psychology.

The gentle social control exercised by the mass media makes use of the spectacles of an undermined private sphere in order to make political processes unrecognizable as such. The depoliticized public realm is dominated by the imposed privatism of mass culture. The personalization of what is public is thus the cement in the cracks of a relatively well-integrated society, which forces suspended conflicts into areas of social psychology. There they are absorbed in categories of deviant behavior: as private conflicts, illness, and crime. These containers now appear to be overflowing. Upgrading the political evaluation of moderately important private conflicts brings to light the cryptopolitical substance of derivative psychic disturbances. This new illumination of regressive phenomena (which does not quite strengthen the movement's capacity for action), however, has been taken by some as an occasion for constructing doctrines of the "new man." I consider such attempts, of which Wilhelm Reich is taken as the progenitor, a symptom, and not the meaning, of the new state of affairs.

The Source of the Protest Potential

The protest potential is clearly generated in bourgeois homes, even if it is only actualized in educational systems and, later, in job situations that contain independent conflict potential. In a necessarily simplified form I should like to discuss two attempts at explanation. The first leads to an interpretation that comprehends the new activism as the expression of a "liberated generation" (Richard W. Flacks). The second suggests an interpretation that lets the young activists appear as representatives of a "fatherless generation" (Alexander Mitscherlich).[2]

1. The Thesis of the Liberated Generation. American studies agree that student activists come from families with privileged status. The family and career orientation of the children is weaker, their academic achievements are generally above average, and their dropout rate is lower. A disproportionately high number of their parents are in the upper middle class, especially from university-trained professional groups. Compared with the parents of conservatively oriented activists they are characterized by higher income, better formal education, urban origin, and a low level of status anxiety and ambition. In addition, these families often possess a tradition of university attendance going back several generations. Relatively frequently, the mothers, too, have attended secondary school or college, and are employed.

The family structure is determined by liberal and egalitarian value-orientations. In these families the typical middle-class life-style seems carried to extremes. The parents' relationship is balanced. They cater to the child's intentions and put a premium on his independence, verbalize and rationally explain their expectations, and punish mainly by withdrawal of love instead of external sanctions. The protest of those among the young who come from such "progressive" homes no longer derives from the familiar, age-old pattern of the bourgeois authority conflict with the strong father. The children tend rather to identify with the mother who sets the example of concern for others and sharpens the sense for the intolerability of repression. One result of an individuating upbringing, in any case, is sensitivity to injury and expressive qualities in interpersonal relations.

The student uprising is thus not a rebellion against parents. There are many indications that the activist young are emphatically committed to "living out expressed but unimplemented parental values."

2. *The Thesis of the Fatherless Generation.* Even if we remain conscious of the inevitable simplification involved in using ideal types, the image of the liberated generation is unsatisfying. It obviously does not account for that segment of students (and especially the non- and ex-students living at the margins of the university) who have belonged to the protest movement from the very beginning. For these Kenneth Kenniston has introduced the expression "culturally alienated." The more the movement has been radicalized, the more this type seems to have gained a growing influence on political action itself. Certain features that have come to define the behavior of precisely the actionistic groups (such as interpretation of situations without adequate information, projective action orientations, strong narcissistic cathexis, and insufficient affect control) can scarcely be explained without relativizing the first socialization type as the limiting case of a typology of patterns of upbringing.

The opposite type comprises students of comparable social origin whose resistance against the burdens of mass college and university study is nevertheless lower. This usually leads to higher dropout rates and poor achievements.

The parents' value-orientations are also more liberal than those of comparable groups but express indecision in the face of a reified pluralism of incompatible values. Childrearing techniques are similarly patterned. They are permissive but contain elements of neglect and do not include attitudes necessary for training in autonomy. Balance in the parents' relationship is disturbed to the point where the mother is the preferred ally in coalitions between children and a single parent. The mother can take on an emphatically solicitous control. The paternal identification model remains vague; the internalization of ideals and norms is rather weak, and the development of superego structures is inhibited. Despite the semblance of liberality, such a pattern of childrearing does not promote an autonomous ego organization. Instead of the New Sensibility we find a new insensibility, which comes to expression most clearly in the inability to act in terms of the other's intentions. A certain narcissism goes hand in hand with the unconcerned instrumentalization of the most sensitive areas of interpersonal intercourse and with the violation of culturally deep-seated taboos—such as that of the integrity of the human body.

The two types of socialization just outlined are limiting cases, modulations of the basic pattern of family structure and childrearing style of certain middle-class groups. This basic pattern probably results from the long-term process of rationalization analyzed by Max Weber. The protest potential seems to emerge most prominently in subcultures in which privatized creeds (and thus the general form in which tradition asserts itself in bourgeois society) have been most permanently shaken.[3] Should future studies confirm these sociopsychological constructions, the two types of the liberated and fatherless generation could help explain the Janus face of youth protest. From the very beginning of the movement emancipatory forces have been connected with regressive ones. This has also rendered the problem of diagnosis more difficult for those theorists who could not avoid seeing in this protest the acceptance of their own critique—a critique which has since become marked by resignation. In West Germany, student protest has found support, or at least sympathy, on the left from old socialist splinter groups to established liberals. The technocrats of protest as an end in itself have set off on the left a process of disintegration, which owes less to consistent strategy than to the ambivalence of the protest potential itself.

What Is to Be Done?

Today this question cannot be answered unequivocally. Only forced interpretations make the present situation seem so clear that answers simply take shape without difficulty. This is the advantage offered by actionism: it generates the illusion that the situation is so unambiguous that only tactical questions are left to be discussed. This reemergence of the neglected "organization problem," however, is not a real advance, but only a bluff. For the prior theoretical problems are not only unsolved but have not even been clearly analyzed and stated.

The protest movement originates at the universities; reforming the universities should be its first, realistic goal. Making the teaching and learning processes dysfunctional is not a tactic that can be rationally defended on political grounds. Instead of using the university for pseudorevolutionary adventures, the movement should aim at creating for it an institutional framework that would make it possible to undo the interlocking of instruction and research with power and privilege inside and outside the university. This would be best served by the democratization of the university, meaning a) that decision-making councils should be opened on all levels to all groups participating in the process of instruction and research and b) that decisions about all questions of practical consequence should come from public discussion and uncompelled decision making in these councils. In this way students, teaching assistants, and junior faculty would obtain the opportunity of setting forth a well-founded, substantive critique of the scientific enterprise, which would reflect on the didactic and methodological presuppositions of instruction and research and demand that the social context of their utilization enter into the basis of their legitimation.

The reorganization of the university in this manner would result in practical consequences for 1) instruction and 2) research as well as for 3) the place of the educational system in society.

1) First, preparation for careers requiring university training would have to free itself from traditional patterns and give way to initiation into critical professional practice. "Critical" means here the combination of competence and learning ability to permit the scrupulous handling of tentative technical knowledge and the context-sensitive, well-informed willingness to resist politically the dubious functional application or control of the knowledge that one practices. The perspective broadens if one thinks not only of future graduates but of the echo that protest has already found today in some university-trained professional groups, who are most directly confronted with the social problems left untouched by the authoritarian welfare state, with its avoidance strategies and rewards. Organizational forms must be found for the realization of practical needs that have hitherto fallen through the mesh of organized group interests.

2) A university divested of its apolitical self-understanding could have an effect in a) preventing research relevant to planning the future from migrating to social sectors outside the university where it is used for repressive ends and b) incorporating the already established and rapidly expanding large-scale research going on outside the university into an overall political decision-making process. If the university were enlightened about the politics of science and were also capable of action, it could make itself an advocate of subjecting alternative evaluations of scientific-technological development to political decisions in consideration of its practical consequences, instead of leaving them to the criteria of the military-industrial complex.

3) If the scientific enterprise were conscious of its political responsibility, it could exert influence on educational

policies. The expansion of the educational system, originally impelled by needs of production, is now coming up against limits. Educational needs cannot be strongly represented by any of the existing organized interest groups, and expansion follows and is restricted by "demand." The question, however, is whether this materialistic compulsion, which can be made transparent to the mass of the population, should not be overcome. The educational system should be able to extend beyond the limit set by the needs of the system of social labor, unless education, a "use value," is to stay subject to the laws of the production of exchange value. If this transformation were to occur, the strict relation between the level of formal education and social status would be loosened, undermining the achievement ideology that is still the basis for the legitimation of status assignment today. That is why a consistently pursued educational policy ought to lead to conflicts that threaten the system.

It is difficult to estimate adequately the order of magnitude of the protest movement. On the one hand, the protagonists' self-estimation seems to me groundless. Students are not a class, they are not even the avant-garde of a class, and they are certainly not leading a revolutionary struggle. In view of the results of actionism, I consider this self-delusion in the grand style pernicious. On the other hand, I would not reject a broad historical perspective. There are several signs indicating that the basis on which the New Sensibility and the zeal of practical reason (including their terrifying deformations) are generated is expanding and that the potential of the youth movement is growing. If this potential does not inhibit itself self-destructively and if we of the older generation do not react without comprehension, it may become the motive force of a long-term process of transformation that prevents foreseeable catastrophes on an international scale and makes possible a measure of emancipation domestically. This cannot be known, but we can encourage it with caution.

Under other historical conditions, the juxtaposition of the categories "revolution" and "reform" constituted a sharp line of demarcation. In industrially advanced societies it no longer discriminates between possible alternative strategies of change. The only way I see to bring about conscious structural change in a social system organized in an authoritarian welfare state is radical reformism. What Marx called critical-revolutionary activity must take this way today. This means that we must promote reforms for clear and publicly discussed goals, even and especially if they have consequences that are incompatible with the mode of production of the established system. The superiority of one mode of production to another cannot become visible under given structural conditions of military technology and strategy as long as economic growth, the production of consumer goods, and the reduction of average labor time—in short, technical progress and private welfare—are the only criteria for comparing competing social systems. However, if we do not deem insignificant the goals, forms, and contents of humane social and communal life, then the superiority of a mode of production can only be measured, in industrial societies, with regard to the scope it opens up for a democratization of decision-making processes in all sectors of society.

CHAPTER FOUR

Technical Progress and the Social Life-World

When C. P. Snow published *The Two Cultures* in 1959, he initiated a discussion of the relation of science and literature which has been going on in other countries as well as in England. Science in this connection has meant the strictly empirical sciences, while literature has been taken more broadly to include methods of interpretation in the cultural sciences. The treatise with which Aldous Huxley entered the controversy, however, *Literature and Science,* does limit itself to confronting the natural sciences with the belles-lettres.

Huxley distinguishes the two cultures primarily according to the specific experiences with which they deal: literature makes statements mainly about private experiences, the sciences about intersubjectively accessible experiences. The latter can be expressed in a formalized language, which can be made universally valid by means of general definitions. In contrast, the language of literature must verbalize what is in principle unrepeatable and must generate an intersubjectivity of mutual understanding in each concrete case. But this distinction between private and public experience allows only a first approximation to the problem. The element of ineffability that literary expression must overcome derives less from a private experience encased in subjectivity than from the constitution of these experiences within the horizon of a life-historical environment. The events whose connection is the object of the law-like hypotheses of the sciences can be described in a spatio-temporal coordinate system, but they do not make up a world:

> The world with which literature deals is the world in which human beings are born and live and finally die; the world in which they love and hate, in which they experience triumph and humiliation, hope and despair; the world of sufferings and enjoyments, of madness and

50

common sense, of silliness, cunning and wisdom; the
world of social pressures and individual impulses, of
reason against passion, of instincts and conventions, of
shared language and unsharable feelings and
sensations . . .[1]

In contrast, science does not concern itself with the contents of
a life-world of this sort, which is culture-bound, ego-centered,
and pre-interpreted in the ordinary language of social groups
and socialized individuals:

> . . . As a professional chemist, say, a professional
> physicist or physiologist, [the scientist] is the inhabitant
> of a radically different universe—not the universe of
> given appearances, but the world of inferred fine
> structures, not the experienced world of unique events
> and diverse qualities, but the world of quantified
> regularities.[2]

Huxley juxtaposes the *social life-world* and the *worldless universe of facts.* He also sees precisely the way in which the
sciences transpose their information about this worldless universe
into the life-world of social groups:

> Knowledge is power and, by a seeming paradox, it is
> through their knowledge of what happens in this
> unexperienced world of abstractions and inferences that
> scientists have acquired their enormous and growing
> power to control, direct, and modify the world of
> manifold appearances in which human beings are
> privileged and condemned to live.[3]

But Huxley does not take up the question of the relation of the two cultures at this juncture, where the sciences
enter the social life-world through the technical exploitation of
their information. Instead he postulates an immediate relation.
Literature should assimilate scientific statements as such, so that
science can take on "flesh and blood."

. . . Until some great artist comes along and tells us
what to do, we shall not know how the muddled words
of the tribe and the too precise words of the textbooks
should be poetically purified, so as to make them capable
of harmonizing our private and unsharable experiences
with the scientific hypotheses in terms of which they
are explained.[4]

This postulate is based, I think, on a misunderstanding.
Information provided by the strictly empirical sciences can be
incorporated in the social life-world only through its technical
utilization, as technological knowledge, serving the expansion
of our power of technical control. Thus, such information is not
on the same level as the action-orienting self-understanding of
social groups. Hence, without mediation, the information content of the sciences cannot be relevant to that part of practical
knowledge which gains expression in literature. It can only
attain significance through the detour marked by the practical
results of technical progress. Taken for itself, knowledge of
atomic physics remains without consequence for the interpretation of our life-world, and to this extent the cleavage between
the two cultures is inevitable. Only when with the aid of
physical theories we can carry out nuclear fission, only when
information is exploited for the development of productive or
destructive forces, can its revolutionary practical results penetrate the literary consciousness of the life-world: poems arise
from consideration of Hiroshima and not from the elaboration
of hypotheses about the transformation of mass into energy.

The idea of an atomic poetry that would elaborate on
hypotheses follows from false premises. In fact, the problematic
relation of literature and science is only one segment of a much
broader problem: *How is it possible to translate technically
exploitable knowledge into the practical consciousness of a
social life-world?* This question obviously sets a new task, not
only or even primarily for literature. The skewed relation of
the two cultures is so disquieting only because, in the seeming
conflict between the two competing cultural traditions, a true
life-problem of scientific civilization becomes apparent: namely,

how can the relation between technical progress and the social life-world, which today is still clothed in a primitive, traditional, and unchosen form, be reflected upon and brought under the control of rational discussion?

To a certain extent practical questions of government, strategy, and administration had to be dealt with through the application of technical knowledge even at an earlier period. Yet today's problem of transposing technical knowledge into practical consciousness has changed not merely its order of magnitude. The mass of technical knowledge is no longer restricted to pragmatically acquired techniques of the classical crafts. It has taken the form of scientific information that can be exploited for technology. On the other hand, behavior-controlling traditions no longer naively define the self-understanding of modern societies. Historicism has broken the natural-traditional validity of action-orienting value systems. Today, the self-understanding of social groups and their worldview as articulated in ordinary language is mediated by the hermeneutic appropriation of traditions as traditions. In this situation questions of life conduct demand a rational discussion that is not focused exclusively either on technical means or on the application of traditional behavioral norms. The reflection that is required extends beyond the production of technical knowledge and the hermeneutical clarification of traditions to the employment of technical means in historical situations whose objective conditions (potentials, institutions, interests) have to be interpreted anew each time in the framework of a self-understanding determined by tradition.

This problem-complex has only entered consciousness within the last two or three generations. In the nineteenth century one could still maintain that the sciences entered the conduct of life through two separate channels: through the technical exploitation of scientific information and through the processes of individual education and culture during academic study. Indeed, in the German university system, which goes back to Humboldt's reform, we still maintain the fiction that the sciences develop their action-orienting power through educational processes within the life history of the individual student. I should like to show that the intention designated by Fichte as a "transformation of knowledge into works" can no longer be carried out in the private sphere of education, but rather can be realized only on the politically relevant level at which technically exploitable knowledge is translatable into the context of our life-world. Though literature participates in this, it is primarily a problem of the sciences themselves.

At the beginning of the nineteenth century, in Humboldt's time, it was still impossible, looking at Germany, to conceive of the scientific transformation of social life. Thus, the university reformers did not have to break seriously with the tradition of practical philosophy. Despite the profound ramifications of revolutions in the political order, the structures of the preindustrial work world persisted, permitting for the last time, as it were, the classical view of the relation of theory to practice. In this tradition, the technical capabilities employed in the sphere of social labor are not capable of immediate direction by theory. They must be pragmatically practiced according to traditional patterns of skill. Theory, which is concerned with the immutable essence of things beyond the mutable region of human affairs, can obtain practical validity only by molding the manner of life of men engaged in theory. Understanding the cosmos as a whole yields norms of individual human behavior, and it is through the actions of the philosophically educated that theory assumes a positive form. This was the only relation of theory to practice incorporated in the traditional idea of university education. Even where Schelling attempts to provide the physician's practice with a scientific basis in natural philosophy, the medical *craft* is unexpectedly transformed into a medical *praxiology*. The physician must orient himself to Ideas derived from natural philosophy in the same way that the subject of moral action orients itself through the Ideas of practical reason.

Since then it has become common knowledge that the scientific transformation of medicine succeeds only to the extent that the pragmatic doctrine of the medical art can be transformed into the control of isolated natural processes, checked by scientific method. The same holds for other areas of social labor. Whether it is a matter of rationalizing the production of goods, management and administration, construction of machine tools, roads, or airplanes, or the manipulation of electoral, consumer, or leisure-time behavior, the professional practice in question will always have to assume the form of technical control of objectified processes.

In the early nineteenth century, the maxim that scientific knowledge is a source of culture required a strict separation between the university and the technical school because the preindustrial forms of professional practice were impervious to theoretical guidance. Today, research processes are coupled with technical conversion and economic exploitation, and production and administration in the industrial system of labor generate feedback for science. The application of science in technology and the feedback of technical progress to research have become the substance of the world of work. In these circumstances, unyielding opposition to the decomposition of the university into specialized schools can no longer invoke the old argument. Today, the reason given for delimiting study on the university model from the professional sphere is not that the latter is still foreign to science, but conversely, that science—to the very extent that it has penetrated professional practice—has estranged itself from humanistic culture. The philosophical conviction of German idealism that scientific knowledge is a source of culture no longer holds for the strictly empirical scientist. It was once possible for theory, via humanistic culture, to become a practical force. Today, theories can become technical power while remaining unpractical, that is, without being expressly oriented to the interaction of a community of human beings. Of course, the sciences now transmit a specific capacity: but the capacity for control, which they teach, is not the same capacity for life and action that was to be expected of the scientifically educated and cultivated.

The cultured possessed orientation in action. Their culture was universal only in the sense of the universality of a culture-bound horizon of a world in which scientific experiences could be interpreted and turned into practical abilities, namely, into a reflected consciousness of the practically necessary. The only type of experience which is admitted as scientific today according to positivistic criteria is not capable of this transposition into practice. The capacity for *control* made possible by the empirical sciences is not to be confused with the capacity for *enlightened action*. But is science, therefore, completely discharged of this task of action-orientation, or does the question of academic education in the framework of a civilization transformed by scientific means arise again today as a problem of the sciences themselves?

First, production processes were revolutionized by scientific methods. Then expectations of technically correct functioning were also transferred to those areas of society that had become independent in the course of the industrialization of labor and thus supported planned organization. The power of technical control over nature made possible by science is extended today directly to society: for every isolatable social system, for every cultural area that has become a separate, closed system whose relations can be analyzed immanently in terms of presupposed system goals, a new discipline emerges in the social sciences. In the same measure, however, the problems of technical control solved by science are transformed into life problems. For the scientific control of natural and social processes—in a word, technology—does not release men from action. Just as before, conflicts must be decided, interests realized, interpretations found—through both action and transaction structured by ordinary language. Today, however, these practical problems are themselves in large measure determined by the system of our technical achievements.

But if technology proceeds from science, and I mean the technique of influencing human behavior no less than that of dominating nature, then the assimilation of this technology into the practical life-world, bringing the technical control of particular areas within the reaches of the communication of acting men, really requires scientific reflection. The prescientific horizon of experience becomes infantile when it naively incorporates contact with the products of the most intensive rationality.

Culture and education can then no longer indeed be restricted to the ethical dimension of personal attitude. Instead, in the political dimension at issue, the theoretical guidance of action must proceed from a scientifically explicated understanding of the world.

The relation of technical progress and social life-world and the translation of scientific information into practical consciousness is not an affair of private cultivation.

I should like to reformulate this problem with reference to political decision-making. In what follows we shall understand "technology" to mean scientifically rationalized control of objectified processes. It refers to the system in which research and technology are coupled with feedback from the economy and administration. We shall understand "democracy" to mean the institutionally secured forms of general and public communication that deal with the practical question of how men can and want to live under the objective conditions of their ever-expanding power of control. Our problem can then be stated as one of the relation of technology and democracy: how can the power of technical control be brought within the range of the consensus of acting and transacting citizens?

I should like first to discuss two antithetical answers. The first, stated in rough outline, is that of Marxian theory. Marx criticizes the system of capitalist production as a power that has taken on its own life in opposition to the interests of productive freedom, of the producers. Through the private form of appropriating socially produced goods, the technical process of producing use values falls under the alien law of an economic process that produces exchange values. Once we trace this self-regulating character of the accumulation of capital back to its origins in private property in the means of production, it becomes possible for mankind to comprehend economic compulsion as an alienated result of its own free productive activity and then abolish it. Finally, the reproduction of social life can be rationally planned as a process of producing use values; society places this process under its technical control. The latter is exercised democratically in accordance with the will and insight of the associated individuals. Here Marx equates the practical insight of a political public with successful technical control. Meanwhile we have learned that even a well-functioning planning bureaucracy with scientific control of the production of goods and services is not a sufficient condition for realizing the associated material and intellectual productive forces in the interest of the enjoyment and freedom of an emancipated society. For Marx did not reckon with the possible emergence at every level of a discrepancy between scientific control of the material conditions of life and a democratic decision-making process. This is the philosophical reason why socialists never anticipated the authoritarian welfare state, where social wealth is relatively guaranteed while political freedom is excluded.

Even if technical control of physical and social conditions for preserving life and making it less burdensome had attained the level that Marx expected would characterize a communist stage of development, it does not follow that they would be linked automatically with social emancipation of the sort intended by the thinkers of the Enlightenment in the eighteenth century and the Young Hegelians in the nineteenth. For the techniques with which the development of a highly industrialized society could be brought under control can no longer be interpreted according to an instrumental model, as though appropriate means were being organized for the realization of goals that are either presupposed without discussion or clarified through communication.

Hans Freyer and Helmut Schelsky have outlined a counter-model which recognizes technology as an independent force. In contrast to the primitive state of technical development, the relation of the organization of means to given or pre-established goals today seems to have been reversed. The process of research and technology—which obeys immanent laws—precipitates in an unplanned fashion new methods for which we then have to find purposeful application. Through progress that has become automatic, Freyer argues, abstract potential continually accrues to us in renewed thrusts. Subsequently, both life interests and fantasy that generates meaning have to take this potential in hand and expend it on concrete goals. Schelsky refines and simplifies this thesis to the point of asserting that technical progress produces not only unforeseen methods but the unplanned goals and applications themselves: technical potentialities command their own practical realization. In particular, he puts forth this thesis with regard to the highly complicated objective exigencies that in political situations allegedly prescribe solutions without alternatives.

> Political norms and laws are replaced by objective
> exigencies of scientific-technical civilization, which
> are not posited as political decisions and cannot be
> understood as norms of conviction or weltanschauung.
> Hence, the idea of democracy loses its classical
> substance, so to speak. In place of the political will
> of the people emerges an objective exigency, which
> man himself produces as science and labor.

In the face of research, technology, the economy, and administration—integrated as a system that has become autonomous—the question prompted by the neohumanistic ideal of culture, namely, how can society possibly exercise sovereignty over the technical conditions of life and integrate them into the practice of the life-world, seems hopelessly obsolete. In the technical state such ideas are suited at best for "the manipulation of motives to help bring about what must happen anyway from the point of view of objective necessity."

It is clear that this thesis of the autonomous character of technical development is not correct. The pace and *direction* of technical development today depend to a great extent on public investments: in the United States the defense and space administrations are the largest sources of research contracts. I suspect that the situation is similar in the Soviet Union. The assertion that politically consequential decisions are reduced to carrying out the immanent exigencies of disposable techniques and that therefore they can no longer be made the theme of practical considerations, serves in the end merely to conceal preexisting, unreflected social interests and prescientific decisions.

As little as we can accept the optimistic convergence of technology and democracy, the pessimistic assertion that technology excludes democracy is just as untenable.

These two answers to the question of how the force of technical control can be made subject to the consensus of acting and transacting citizens are inadequate. Neither of them can deal appropriately with the problem with which we are objectively confronted in the West and East, namely, how we can actually bring under control the preexisting, unplanned relations of technical progress and the social life-world. The tensions between productive forces and social intentions that Marx diagnosed and whose explosive character has intensified in an unforeseen manner in the age of thermonuclear weapons are the consequence of an ironic relation of theory to practice. The direction of technical progress is still largely determined today by social interests that arise autochthonously out of the compulsion of the reproduction of social life without being reflected upon and confronted with the declared political self-understanding of social groups. In consequence, new technical capacities erupt without preparation into existing forms of life-activity and conduct. New potentials for expanded power of technical control make obvious the disproportion between the results of the most organized rationality and unreflected goals, rigidified value systems, and obsolete ideologies.

Today, in the industrially most advanced systems, an energetic attempt must be made consciously to take in hand the mediation between technical progress and the conduct of life in the major industrial societies, a mediation that has previously taken place without direction, as a mere continuation of natural history. This is not the place to discuss the social, economic, and political conditions on which a long-term central research policy would have to depend. It is not enough for a social system to fulfill the conditions of technical rationality. Even if the cybernetic dream of a virtually instinctive self-stabilization could be realized, the value system would have contracted in the meantime to a set of rules for the maximization of power and comfort; it would be equivalent to the biological base value of survival at any cost, that is, ultrastability.

Through the unplanned sociocultural consequences of technological progress, the human species has challenged itself to learn not merely to affect its social destiny, but to control it. This challenge of technology cannot be met with technology alone. It is rather a question of setting into motion a politically effective discussion that rationally brings the social potential constituted by technical knowledge and ability into a defined and controlled relation to our practical knowledge and will. On the one hand, such discussion could enlighten those who act politically about the tradition-bound self-understanding of their interests in relation to what is technically possible and feasible. On the other hand, they would be able to judge practically, in the light of their now articulated and newly interpreted needs, the direction and the extent to which they want to develop technical knowledge for the future.

This *dialectic of potential and will* takes place today without reflection in accordance with interests for which public justification is neither demanded nor permitted. Only if we could elaborate this dialectic with political consciousness could we succeed in directing the mediation of technical progress and the conduct of social life, which until now has occurred as an extension of natural history; its conditions being left outside the framework of discussion and planning. The fact that this is a matter for reflection means that it does not belong to the professional competence of specialists. The substance of domination is not dissolved by the power of technical control. To the contrary, the former can simply hide behind the latter. The irrationality of domination, which today has become a collective peril to life, could be mastered only by the development of a political decision-making process tied to the principle of general discussion free from domination. Our only hope for the rationalization of the power structure lies in conditions that favor political power for thought developing through dialogue. The redeeming power of reflection cannot be supplanted by the extension of technically exploitable knowledge.

CHAPTER FIVE

The Scientization of Politics
and Public Opinion

The scientization of politics is not yet a reality, but it is a real tendency for which there is evidence: the scope of research under government contract and the extent of scientific consultation to public services are primary examples. From the beginning the modern state, which arose from the need for central financial administration in connection with the market patterns of an emerging national and territorial economy, was dependent on the expertise of officials trained in the law. However, their technical knowledge did not differ fundamentally in form from professional knowledge of the sort possessed by the military. Just as the latter had to organize standing armies, so the officials had to organize a permanent administration. Both were practicing an art more than applying a science. It is only recently that bureaucrats, the military, and politicians have been orienting themselves to strictly scientific recommendations in the exercise of their public functions—indeed, this practice has only existed on a large scale since World War II. This marks a new or second stage of that "rationalization" which Max Weber had already comprehended as the basis for the development of bureaucratic domination. It is not as though scientists had seized state power; but the exercise of power domestically and its assertion against external enemies are no longer rationalized only through the mediation of administrative activity organized through the division of labor, regulated according to differentiated responsibilities, and linked to instituted norms. Instead they have been structurally transformed by the objective exigencies of new technologies and strategies.

Following a tradition that goes back to Hobbes, Weber found clear definitions for the relation of expertise and political practice. His famous confrontation of administration by officials versus political leadership served to separate strictly the functions of the expert from those of the politician.[1] The latter makes use of technical knowledge, but the practice of self-assertion and domination requires in addition that a person or group with specific interests make decisions and carry them out. In the last analysis political action cannot rationally justify its own premises. Instead a decision is made between competing value orders and convictions, which escape compelling arguments and remain inaccessible to cogent discussion. As much as the objective knowledge of the expert may determine the techniques of rational administration and military security and thereby subject the means of political practice to scientific rules, practical decision in concrete situations cannot be *sufficiently* legitimated through reason. Rationality in the choice of means accompanies avowed irrationality in orientation to values, goals, and needs. According to Weber only complete division of labor between the objectively informed and technically schooled general staffs of the bureaucracy and the military on the one hand and leaders with a power instinct and intense will on the other will make possible the scientization of politics.

Today we are confronted with the question whether this *decisionistic model* is valid for the second stage of the rationalization of domination. Systems analysis and especially decision theory do not merely make new technologies available, thus improving traditional instruments; they also rationalize choice as such by means of calculated strategies and automatic decision procedures. To this extent the objective necessity disclosed by the specialists seems to assert itself over the leaders' decisions.

Following a tradition that extends back through Saint-Simon to Bacon, the decisionistic definition of the relation of expertise to political practice is being abandoned by many in favor of a *technocratic model*.[2] The dependence of the professional on the politician appears to have reversed itself. The latter becomes the mere agent of a scientific intelligentsia, which, in concrete circumstances, elaborates the objective implications and requirements of available techniques and resources as well as of optimal strategies and rules of control. If it is possible to rationalize decisions about practical questions, as a choice in situations of uncertainty, to the point where the "symmetry of uncertainty" (Rittel) and thus the problems of decision in general are reduced step by step, then the politician in the technical state is left with nothing but a fictitious decision-making power. The politician would then be at best something like a stopgap in a still imperfect rationalization of power, in which the initiative has in any case passed to scientific analysis and technical planning. The state seems forced to abandon the substance of power in favor of an efficient way of applying available techniques in the framework of strategies that are objectively called for. It appears to be no longer an apparatus for the forcible realization of interests that have no foundation in principle and can only be answered for decisionistically. It becomes instead the organ of thoroughly rational administration.

But the weaknesses of this technocratic model are evident. On the one hand, it assumes an immanent necessity of technical progress, which owes its appearance of being an independent, self-regulating process only to the way in which social interests operate in it—namely through continuity with unreflected, unplanned, passively adaptive natural history.[3] On the other hand, this model presupposes a continuum of rationality in the treatment of technical and practical problems, which cannot in fact exist.[4] For the new methods that characterize the rationalization of power in its second stage do not bring about the disappearance of the problem-complex connected with the decision of practical issues. Within the framework of research operations that expand our power of technical control we can make no cogent statements about "value systems," that is, about social needs and objective states of consciousness, about the directions of emancipation and regression. Either there are still other forms of decision than the theoretical-technical for the rational clarification of practical issues that cannot be completely answered by technologies and strategies, or no reasons can be given for decisions in such issues. In that case we would have to return to the decisionistic model.

This conclusion has been drawn by Hermann Lübbe:

> Whereas the politician once was respected more than
> the expert because the latter merely knew and planned
> what the former knew how to carry out, the situation
> has now been reversed. For the expert knows how to
> understand what is prescribed by the logic of real
> conditions, while the politician takes positions in
> conflict situations for which there is no court of earthly
> reason.[5]

Lübbe incorporates the new stage of rationalization into the
decisionistic model. But he maintains the antithesis between
technical knowledge and the exercise of political power as
defined by Weber and Carl Schmitt. He reproaches the technocratic self-understanding of the new experts with camouflaging
what is really as political as ever with the "logic of reality."
True, the scope of pure decision has been restricted to the degree that the politician disposes of an augmented and more
refined arsenal of technical means and can make use of aids to
strategic decision. But within this confined area what decisionism
always presupposed has now become true for the first time.
Only now has the problem-complex of political decisions been
reduced to a core that simply cannot be rationalized any further.
Calculation by decision procedures, when carried to extremes,
reduces the decision itself to its pure form, purging it of every
element that could be made accessible in any way to cogent
analysis.

In this respect, however, the *expanded decisionistic
model* has lost none of its original dubiousness. To be sure, it
has descriptive value for the practice of scientifically informed
decisions as they are made today in the centers of command in
the mass democracies, prototypically in the United States. But
this does not mean that there are logical reasons why this type
of decision must be withdrawn from further reflection. Rationalization may in fact be discontinued at the gaps in politically
directed technological-strategic research and replaced by deci-

sions. If so, it is a noteworthy social fact explicable on the basis of objective constellations of interests. But it is not something that necessarily follows from the nature of the real problems, unless scientific discussion or any disciplined consideration going beyond the bounds of the positivistically approved mode of discourse is to be excluded from the very beginning. Since this is not the case, we can observe that the decisionistic model, however much it approximates the actual procedures of scientized politics, is inadequate according to its own theoretical claims. For there is obviously an interdependence between values that proceed from interest situations and techniques that can be utilized for the satisfaction of value-oriented needs. If so-called values in the long run lose their connection with the technically appropriate satisfaction of real needs, they become functionless and die out as ideologies. Inversely, new values can develop from new techniques in changed interest situations. In both cases, the decisionistic separation of questions of value and life from those of objective necessity remains abstract. The possibility that the introduction of continually augmented and improved techniques does not merely remain bound to undiscussed value orientations but also subjects traditional values to a sort of pragmatic corroboration was discussed some time ago by Dewey. Ultimately, in this view, value convictions are supposed to persist only to the extent that they can be controllably connected to available and imaginable techniques, that is, to the possible realization of value by producing goods or changing situations. True, Dewey did not take into account the difference between the control of technical recommendations by means of their results and the practical confirmation of techniques in the hermeneutically clarified context of concrete situations. Nevertheless, he insisted on the pragmatic examination and consequently the rational discussion of the relation between available techniques and practical decisions. This relation is ignored by the decisionists' viewpoint.

In the *pragmatistic model* the strict separation between the function of the expert and the politician is replaced by a critical interaction. This interaction not only strips the ideologically supported exercise of power of an unreliable basis of legitimation but makes it accessible *as a whole* to scientifically informed discussion, thereby substantially changing it. Despite the technocratic view, experts have not become sovereign over politicians subjected to the demands of the facts and left with a purely fictitious power of decision. Nor, despite the implications of the decisionistic model, does the politician retain a preserve outside of the necessarily rationalized areas of practice in which practical problems are decided upon as ever by acts of the will. Rather, reciprocal communication seems possible and necessary, through which scientific experts advise the decision-makers and politicians consult scientists in accordance with practical needs. Thus, on the one hand the development of new techniques is governed by a horizon of needs and historically determined interpretations of these needs, in other words, of value systems. This horizon has to be made explicit. On the other hand, these social interests, as reflected in the value systems, are regulated by being tested with regard to the technical possibilities and strategic means for their gratification. In this manner they are partly confirmed, partly rejected, articulated, and reformulated, or denuded of their ideologically transfigured and compelling character.

So far we have considered the three models of the relation of expertise and politics without reference to the structure of modern mass democracy. Only one of them, the pragmatistic, is necessarily related to democracy. If the division of power and responsibility between experts and leaders is carried out according to the decisionistic pattern, then the politically functioning public realm of the citizenry can serve only to legitimate the ruling group. The election and confirmation of governing individuals, or those capable of governing, are as a rule plebiscitary acts. The reason that democratic choice takes the form of acclamation rather than public discussion is that choice applies only to those who occupy positions with decision-making power and not to the guidelines of future decisions themselves. At best these decision-makers legitimate themselves before the public. Decisions themselves, according to the decisionistic view, must remain basically beyond public discussion. The scientization of politics then automatically accords with the theory developed by Weber, extended by Schumpeter, and now unquestioned by modern political sociology, a theory that in the last analysis reduces the process of democratic decision-making to a regulated acclamation procedure for elites alternately appointed to exercise power. In this way power, untouched in its irrational substance, can be legitimated but not rationalized.

The claim to rationalization, in contrast, is upheld by the technocratic model of scientized politics. Of course, the reduction of political power to rational administration can be conceived here only at the expense of democracy itself. If politicians were strictly subjected to objective necessity, a politically functioning public could at best legitimate the administrative personnel and judge the professional qualifications of salaried officials. But if the latter were of comparable qualifications it would in principle be a matter of indifference which competing elite group obtained power. A technocratic administration of industrial society would deprive any democratic decision-making process of its object. This conclusion has been drawn by Helmut Schelsky:

> . . . the people's political will is supplanted by the objective exigencies that man produces as science and labor.[6]

In contrast, the successful transposition of technical and strategic recommendations into practice is, according to the pragmatistic model, increasingly dependent on mediation by the public as a political institution. Communication between experts and the agencies of political decision determines the direction of technical progress on the basis of the tradition-bound self-understanding of practical needs. Inversely it measures and criticizes this self-understanding in the light of the possibilities for gratification created by technology. Such communication must therefore necessarily be rooted in social interests and in the value-orientations of a given social life-world. In both directions the feedback-monitored communication process is grounded in what Dewey called "value beliefs." That is, it is based on a historically determined preunderstanding, governed by social norms, of what is practically necessary in a concrete situation. This preunderstanding is a consciousness that can only be enlightened hermeneutically, through articulation in the discourse of citizens in a community. Therefore the communication provided for in the pragmatistic model, which is supposed to render political practice scientific, cannot occur independently of the communication that is always already in process on the prescientific level. The latter type of communication, however, can be institutionalized in the democratic form of public discussions among the citizen body. The relation of the *sciences* to *public opinion* is constitutive for the scientization of politics.

It is true that this relation has never been made explicit in the tradition of pragmatistic thought. For Dewey it seemed self-evident that the relation of reciprocal guidance and enlightenment between the production of techniques and strategies on the one hand and the value-orientations of interested groups on the other could be realized within the unquestionable horizon of common sense and an uncomplicated public realm. But the *structural change in the bourgeois public realm* would have demonstrated the naïveté of this view even if it were not already invalidated by the internal development of the sciences. For the latter have made a basically unsolved problem out of the appropriate translation of technical information even between individual disciplines, let alone between the sciences and the public at large. Anyone who adheres to the notion of permanent communication between the sciences, considered in terms of their political relevance, and informed public opinion becomes suspect of wanting to put scientific discussion on a mass basis and thus to misuse it ideologically. This position in turn provokes a critique of ideology that opposes the simplified and overextended interpretation of scientific results in accordance with a weltanschauung, and instead firmly insists upon the positivistic separation of theory and practice. Weber's thesis of the neutrality of the sciences with regard to preexisting practical valuations can be convincingly employed against illusionary rationalizations of political problems, against *short-circuiting* the connection between technical expertise and a public that can be influenced by manipulation, and against the distorted response which scientific information meets with in a deformed public realm.[7]

Nevertheless, as soon as this critique calls into question a more extensive rationalization of the power structure as such, it succumbs to the limitations of positivism and to an ideology that makes science impervious to self-reflection. For then it confuses the actual difficulty of effecting permanent communication between science and public opinion with the violation of logical and methodological rules. True, as it stands the pragmatistic model cannot be applied to political decision-making in modern mass democracies. However, this is not because discussing practical questions both with reference to available techniques and strategies and within the horizon of the explicated self-understanding of a social life-world would require the illusory rationalization of unfounded acts of will. The reason is rather that this model neglects the specific logical characteristics and the social preconditions for the reliable translation of scientific information into the ordinary language of practice and inversely for a translation from the context of practical questions back into the specialized language of technical and strategic recommendations.[8] The example of the United States, the country in which the scientization of political practice has progressed the furthest, shows how such hermeneutic tasks arise in the discussion between scientists and politicians and how they are solved without their becoming conscious as such. This tacit hermeneutic is not explicitly subjected to scientific discipline, and only therefore does it seem, both externally and in the self-understanding of those involved, that there is a logically necessary division of labor between technical consultation and enlightened decision.

Communication between politically authorized contracting agencies and objectively knowledgeable and competent scientists at major research and consulting organizations marks the critical zone of the translation of practical questions into scientifically formulated questions and the translation of scientific information back into answers to practical questions. Of

SCIENTIZATION OF POLITICS/PUBLIC OPINION   71

course this statement does not really capture the dialectic of the process. The Heidelberg Research Project in Systems Analysis has reported a revealing example. The headquarters of the U.S. Air Force using experienced contact men presents a roughly outlined problem of military technology or organization to the program department of a research and consulting organization. The starting point is a vaguely formulated need. A more rigorous version of the problem first arises during the course of protracted communication between officers, themselves scientifically trained, and the project director. But contact is not broken off once the real problem is identified and successfully defined, for this suffices only to conclude a detailed contract. During the research itself, information is exchanged at all levels, from the president of the research organization down to the technician, with the corresponding personnel at the contracting institution. Communication may not end until the solution of the problem has basically been found, for only when the solution can be foreseen in principle is the goal of the project ultimately defined. The preunderstanding of the problem—the practical need of the contracting agency—is articulated in the measure that theoretical solutions, and consequently techniques of execution, crystallize in rigorously constructed models. The communication between the two partners is like a net of rational discussion stretching between practice and science. It must not break if during the development of specific technologies or strategies the originally vague, preunderstood interest in the elimination of a problematic situation is not to be frustrated—if instead its intention is to be preserved in formalized scientific models.

Inversely, practical needs, corresponding goals, and value systems themselves also become specific and determinate only in relation to their technically possible realization. The understanding that social groups engaged in political action have of their situation is so dependent on the techniques available for the realization of interests that research projects are often not motivated by practical problems but instead brought to the attention of politicians by scientists. Given knowledge of the state of research, techniques can be projected for which connections with practical needs then have to be sought or for which connections with newly articulated needs have to be created. However, up to this point in problem-solving and the articulation of needs, only one-half of the process of translation has been covered. The technically appropriate solution of a problematic situation that has been brought to consciousness in a precise manner must in turn be translated back into the totality of the historical situation in which it has practical consequences. Ultimately, the evaluation of completed systems and evolved strategies requires the same form of interpreting a concrete situation with which the translation process began in the preunderstanding of the initial practical situation.

The process of translation that has become customary between political authorities that grant contracts and the consultants has also been institutionalized on a large scale. At the governmental level bureaucracies to direct research and development and scientific consulting agencies have been set up. Their function again reflects the singular dialectic of the transposition of science into political practice. In the framework of these agencies permanent communication between science and politics is established. Otherwise it could only arise *ad hoc* with the granting of special research commissions. The first government committee for scientists, founded by President Roosevelt in 1940, shortly before America entered the war, assumed the two functions now fulfilled by a large consulting apparatus. Political consultation has two tasks. The first is to interpret the results of research within the horizon of guiding interests that determine the political actors' understanding of their situation. The second is to evaluate projects and to stimulate and choose programs that orient the process of research in the direction of practical issues.

As soon as this task is taken out of the context of individual problems and the development of research as a whole is considered, the real problem of the dialogue between science and politics reveals itself to be the formulation of a long-term research policy. This would be the attempt to bring under control the traditional, fortuitous unplanned relations between technical progress and the social life-world. The direction of technical progress today is still largely determined by social

interests that arise spontaneously from the compulsion to repro-
duce social life; they are not reflected as such and confronted
with the declared political self-understanding of social groups.
Consequently new technical potentials intrude unprepared into
existing forms of life conduct. They only make more evident the
disproportion between the results of the most intensive rationality and unreflected goals, petrified value systems, and obsolete
ideologies. The advisory bodies concerned with research policy
give rise to a new type of interdisciplinary, future-oriented research, which ought to clarify the immanent developmental state
and social preconditions of technical progress in connection
with the cultural and educational level of society as a whole.
They would thus offer a viewpoint different from that bounded
by preexisting, unreflected social interests. These investigations,
too, obey a hermeneutic interest in knowledge. For they make it
possible to confront given social institutions and their self-
understanding with the technology that is actually used and
potentially available. Inversely, as part of this projected clarification by means of the critique of ideology, they make it possible
to reorient social needs and declared goals. The formulation of
a long-term research policy, the preparation of new industries
that utilize future scientific information, and the planning of an
educational system for a qualified younger generation whose
jobs are yet to be created are part of an endeavor to direct
consciously what has previously taken place spontaneously and
without planning: the mediation of technological progress with
the conduct of life in large industrial societies. This endeavor
embodies the dialectic of enlightened will and self-conscious
potential.

The communication between experts at major research
and consulting organizations and political authorities about individual projects takes place within an objectively delimited
problem area, and discussion between consulting scientists and
the government remains bound to the constellation of given
situations and available potentials. But for this third task of
programming social development as a whole, the dialogue between scientists and politicians is freed from the influence of
specific problems. It must of course link up to a concrete situa-

tion, namely to a historical phase of tradition and to concrete social interests on the one hand, and to a given level of technical knowledge and industrial utilization on the other. Beyond this, however, the attempt at a long-term research and education policy oriented to immanent possibilities and objective consequences must be left up to the dialectic which we have become acquainted with in its earlier phases. It must enlighten those who take political action about their tradition-bound self-understanding of their interests and goals in relation to socially potential technical knowledge and capacity. At the same time it must put them in a position to judge practically, in the light of these articulated and newly interpreted needs, in what direction they want to develop their technical knowledge and capacity in the future. This discussion necessarily moves within a circle. For only to the extent that, knowing the technical potential of our historically determined will, we orient ourselves to the given situation, can we know in turn what specifically oriented expansion of our technical potential we want for the future.

In the last analysis the process of translation between science and politics is related to public opinion. This relation is not external to it, as though it were a question of taking prevailing constitutional norms into account. Rather it follows immanently and necessarily from the requirements of the confrontation of *technical knowledge and capacity* with *tradition-bound self-understanding*. The latter forms the horizon within which needs are interpreted as goals and goals are hypostatized as values. An element of anticipation is always contained in the integration of technical knowledge and the hermeneutical process of arriving at self-understanding. For it is set in motion by discussion among scientists isolated from the citizenry. The enlightenment of a scientifically instrumented political will according to standards of rationally binding discussion can proceed only from the horizon of communicating citizens themselves and must lead back to it. The consultants who would like to find out what will is expressed by political organizations are equally subject to the hermeneutic constraint of participating in the historical self-understanding of a social group—in the last analysis, in the conversations of citizens. Such an explication is, of course, bound to the methods of the hermeneutic sciences. But the latter do not destroy the dogmatic core of traditional, historically generated interpretations, they only clarify them. The two additional steps of employing the social sciences to analyze this self-understanding in connection with social interests on the one hand, and of ascertaining available techniques and strategies on the other lead beyond this area of public discourse. But the result of these steps, as the enlightenment of political will, can become effective only within the communication of citizens. For the articulation of needs in accordance with technical knowledge can be ratified exclusively *in the consciousness of the political actors themselves*. Experts cannot delegate to themselves this act of confirmation from those who have to account with their life histories for new interpretations of social needs and for accepted means of mastering problematic situations. With this reservation, however, the experts must anticipate the act of confirmation. Insofar as they assume this representative role, the experts necessarily think within the context of the philosophy of history, but in an experimental way and without being able to share the teleology and dogma of the tradition.

While integrating technology into the hermeneutically explicated self-understanding of a given situation, the process of the scientization of politics could be realized only if we had the guarantee that political will had obtained the enlightenment it wanted and simultaneously that enlightenment had permeated existing political will as much as it could under given, desired, and controllable circumstances. This could be guaranteed only by the ideal conditions of general communication extending to the entire public and free from domination. These considerations of principle must not, however, disguise the fact that the empirical conditions for the application of the pragmatistic model are lacking. The depoliticization of the mass of the population and the decline of the public realm as a political institution are components of a system of domination that tends to exclude practical questions from public discussion. The bureaucratized exercise of power has its counterpart in a public realm confined to spectacles and acclamation. This takes care of the approval of a mediatized population.[9] But even if we disregard the limits established by the existing system and assume that a social basis could be found today for public discussion among a broad public, the provision of relevant scientific information would still not be simple.

Leaving aside the public's ability to respond, the very results of research that are of the greatest practical consequence are the most inaccessible. While earlier industrially utilizable information was sometimes kept secret or protected for reasons of economic competition, today the free flow of information is blocked primarily by regulations of military secrecy. The interval between discovery and public disclosure for strategically relevant findings is at least three years and in many cases more than a decade.

There is an additional barrier between science and public knowledge that disturbs the flow of communication on the most basic level: the bureaucratic encapsulation that arises from the organization of the modern research process. Along with the forms of individual scholarship and an unproblematic unity of research and teaching, the unconstrained and formerly automatic contact of the individual scientist with the larger public, whether of students or of educated laymen, has disappeared. The concrete, objective interest of the scientist integrated into a large organization, aimed at the solution of narrowly circumscribed problems, no longer needs to be coupled from the beginning with a teacher's or publicist's concern with the transmission of knowledge to a public of auditors or readers. For the client at the gates of organized research, to whom scientific information is addressed, is now no longer (at least immediately) a public engaged in learning or discussion. It is instead a contracting agency interested in the outcome of the research process for the sake of its technical application. Formerly the task of literary presentation belonged to scientific reflection itself. In the system of large-scale research it is replaced by the memorandum formulated in relation to the contract and the research report aimed at technical recommendations.

Of course, there has grown up an esoteric scientific public in which experts exchange knowledge through professional journals or at conferences. But one would scarcely have expected to see contacts established between it and the literary, let alone political public, even if a singular difficulty had not necessitated a new form of communication. It has been calculated that the differentiation of research during the past one hundred years has doubled the number of professional and technical journals every fifteen years. Today, fifty thousand scientific journals are put out around the globe.[10] With the rising flood of information that the scientific community has to deal with, attempts multiply to summarize the material, which is increasingly difficult to survey, and to order and process it to make an overview possible.

Journals of abstracts and reports are the first step in the direction of a process of translation that transforms and refines the raw material of original information. A number of journals serve the same purpose of communication between scientists of different disciplines who need an interpreter to be able to employ important information in neighboring fields for their own work. The more specialized research becomes, the greater the distances that important information must traverse in order to enter into the work of another expert. Physicists may even use *Time Magazine* to inform themselves about new developments in technology and chemistry. Helmut Krauch is undoubtedly right in suspecting that in Germany, too, interchange among scientists is already dependent on scientific journalism extending from elaborately written reports to the scientific columns of the daily press.[11] Cybernetics, which has developed its models on the basis of processes in physiology and communications technology, neuropsychology, and economics, thus connecting findings of the most remote disciplines, is a good example of how important it is to keep communication channels open even if information from one specialist to another has to take the long route of ordinary language and the everyday understanding of the layman. Given a high degree of division of labor, the lay public often provides the shortest path of internal understanding between mutually estranged specialists. But this necessity for the translation of scientific information, which grows out of the needs of the research process itself, also benefits the endangered communication between scientists and the general public in the political sphere.

An additional tendency that counters the communication block between the two areas results from the international pressure for the peaceful coexistence of competing social systems. As Oskar Morgenstein has shown, military secrecy regulations, which inhibit the free flow of information in the public realm, become increasingly less compatible with the conditions of armament control, which becomes ever more urgent.[12] The growing risks of a precarious balance of deterrence necessitate reciprocally controlled disarmament. And the comprehensive inspection system that this presupposes can work effectively only if the principle of public accessibility is extended rigorously to international relations, strategic plans, and, above all, to militarily employable potentials. The core of this potential is strategically utilizable research itself. The program of an Open World thus demands in the first instance the free exchange of scientific information. Under the aegis of a general arms race, state monopolization of the technologically productive sciences is around the corner. Given the needs of information exchange, there is some evidence that this monopolization may be regarded as a transitional phase on the way to the collective utilization of information on the basis of unrestricted communication between science and the public realm.

However, neither the inner scientific requirement of translation nor the external requirement of free exchange of research information would actually suffice to set in motion a discussion of the practical consequences of scientific results among a responsive public, if the responsible scientists themselves did not ultimately take the initiative. The third tendency that we should like to adduce in favor of such discussion arises from the role conflict in which representative scientists become involved as scientists on the one hand and citizens on the other. To the extent that the sciences are really taken into the service of political practice, scientists are objectively compelled to go beyond the technical recommendations that they produce and reflect upon their practical consequences. This was especially and dramatically true for the atomic physicists involved in the production of the atomic and hydrogen bombs.

Since then there have been discussions in which leading scientists have argued about the political ramifications of their research practice, such as the damages that radioactive fallout have caused to the present health of the population and to the genetic substance of the human species. But the examples are few and far between. They show at least that responsible scientists, disregarding their professional or official roles, cross the boundaries of their inner scientific world and address themselves directly to public opinion when they want either to avert practical consequences connected with the choice of specific technologies or to criticize specific research investments in terms of their social effects.

Nevertheless, one would scarcely know from these small beginnings that the discussion that has begun in the offices of scientific consultants to government agencies basically has to be transferred to the broader political forum of the general public. The same holds for the dialogue now going on between scientists and politicians about the formulation of a long-term research policy.

As we have seen, the preconditions are unfavorable on both sides. On the one hand we can no longer reckon with functioning institutions for public discussion among the general public. On the other, the specialization of large-scale research and a bureaucratized apparatus of power reinforce each other only too well while the public is excluded as a political force. The choice that interests us is not between one elite that effectively exploits vital resources of knowledge over the heads of a mediatized population and another that is isolated from inputs of scientific information, so that technical knowledge flows inadequately into the process of political decision-making. The question is rather whether a productive body of knowledge is merely transmitted to men engaged in technical manipulation for purposes of control or is simultaneously appropriated as the linguistic possession of communicating individuals. A scientized society could constitute itself as a rational one only to the extent that science and technology are mediated with the conduct of life through the minds of its citizens.

There is a special dimension in which the controlled translation of technical into practical knowledge and thus the scientifically guided rationalization of political power is possible. Political rationalization occurs through the enlightenment of political will, correlated with instruction about its technical potential. This dimension is evaded when such enlightenment is considered either impossible because of the need for authoritative decisions or superfluous because of technocracy. In both cases, the objective consequences would be the same: a premature halt to possible rationalization. And the illusory attempts of the technocrats to have political decisions be directed only by the logic of objective exigency would justify the decisionists by leaving sheerly arbitrary what remains an irreducible remnant of practice on the periphery of technological rationality.

CHAPTER SIX

Technology and Science as "Ideology"

For Herbert Marcuse on his seventieth birthday,
July 19, 1968

Max Weber introduced the concept of "rationality" in order to define the form of capitalist economic activity, bourgeois private law, and bureaucratic authority. Rationalization means, first of all, the extension of the areas of society subject to the criteria of rational decision. Second, social labor is industrialized, with the result that criteria of instrumental action also penetrate into other areas of life (urbanization of the mode of life, technification of transport and communication). Both trends exemplify the type of purposive-rational action, which refers to either the organization of means or choice between alternatives. Planning can be regarded as purposive-rational action of the second order. It aims at the establishment, improvement, or expansion of systems of purposive-rational action themselves.

The progressive "rationalization" of society is linked to the institutionalization of scientific and technical development. To the extent that technology and science permeate social institutions and thus transform them, old legitimations are destroyed. The secularization and "disenchantment" of action-orienting worldviews, of cultural tradition as a whole, is the obverse of the growing "rationality" of social action.

Herbert Marcuse has taken these analyses as a point of departure in order to demonstrate that the formal concept of rationality—which Weber derived from the purposive-rational action of the capitalist entrepreneur, the industrial wage laborer, the abstract legal person, and the modern administrative official and based on the criteria of science as well as technology—has specific substantive implications. Marcuse is convinced that what Weber called "rationalization" realizes not rationality as such but rather, in the name of rationality, a specific form of unacknowledged political domination. Because this sort of rationality extends to the correct choice among strategies, the appropriate application of technologies, and the efficient establishment of systems (with *presupposed* aims in *given* situations), it removes the total social framework of interests in which strategies are chosen, technologies applied, and systems established, from the scope of reflection and rational reconstruction. Moreover, this rationality extends only to relations of possible technical control and therefore requires a type of action that implies domination, whether of nature or of society. By virtue of its structure, purposive-rational action is the exercise of control. That is why, in accordance with this rationality, the "rationalization" of the conditions of life is synonymous with the institutionalization of a form of domination whose political character becomes unrecognizable: the technical reason of a social system of purposive-rational action does not lose its political content. Marcuse's critique of Weber comes to the conclusion that

> the very concept of technical reason is perhaps ideological. Not only the application of technology but technology itself is domination (of nature and men)— methodical, scientific, calculated, calculating control. Specific purposes and interests of domination are not foisted upon technology "subsequently" and from the outside; they enter the very construction of the technical apparatus. Technology is always a historical-social *project:* in it is projected what a society and its ruling interests intend to do with men and things. Such a "purpose" of domination is "substantive" and to this extent belongs to the very form of technical reason.[1]

As early as 1956 Marcuse referred in a quite different context to the peculiar phenomenon that in industrially advanced capitalist societies domination tends to lose its exploitative and oppressive character and become "rational," without political domination thereby disappearing: "domination is dependent only on the capacity and drive to maintain and extend the apparatus as a whole."[2] Domination is rational in that a system can be maintained which can allow itself to make the growth of the forces of production, coupled with scientific and technical progress, the basis of its legitimation although, at the same time, the level of the productive forces constitutes a potential in relation to which "the renunciations and burdens placed on individuals seem more and more unnecessary and irrational."[3] In Marcuse's judgment, the objectively superfluous repression can be recognized in the "intensified subjection of individuals to the enormous apparatus of production and distribution, in the deprivatization of free time, in the almost indistinguishable fusion of constructive and destructive social labor."[4] Paradoxically, however, this repression can disappear from the consciousness of the population because the legitimation of domination has assumed a new character: it refers to the "constantly increasing productivity and domination of nature which keeps individuals . . . living in increasing comfort."[5]

The institutionalized growth of the forces of production following from scientific and technical progress surpasses all historical proportions. From it the institutional framework draws its opportunity for legitimation. The thought that relations of production can be measured against the potential of developed productive forces is prevented because the existing relations of production present themselves as the technically necessary organizational form of a rationalized society. Here "rationality," in Weber's sense, shows its Janus face. It is no longer only a critical standard for the developmental level of the forces of production in relation to which the objectively superfluous, repressive character of historically obsolete relations of production can be exposed. It is also an apologetic standard through which these same relations of production can be justified as a functional institutional framework. Indeed, in relation to its apologetic serviceability, "rationality" is weakened as a critical standard and degraded to a corrective *within* the sys-

tem: what can still be said is at best that society is "poorly pro-
grammed." At the stage of their scientific-technical development,
then, the forces of production appear to enter a new constellation with the relations of production. Now they no longer
function as the basis of a critique of prevailing legitimations in
the interest of political enlightenment, but become instead the
basis of legitimation. *This* is what Marcuse conceives of as
world-historically new.

But if this is the case, must not the rationality embodied
in systems of purposive-rational action be understood as specifically limited? Must not the rationality of science and technology, instead of being reducible to unvarying rules of logic
and method have absorbed a substantive, historically derived,
and therefore transitory a priori structure? Marcuse answers in
the affirmative:

> The principles of modern science were *a priori*
> structured in such a way that they could serve as
> conceptual instruments for a universe of self-propelling,
> productive control; theoretical operationalism came to
> correspond to practical operationalism. The scientific
> method which led to the ever-more-effective domination
> of nature thus came to provide the pure concepts as
> well as the instrumentalities for the ever-more-effective
> domination of man by man *through* the domination of
> nature . . . Today, domination perpetuates and extends
> itself not only through technology but *as* technology,
> and the latter provides the great legitimation of the
> expanding political power, which absorbs all spheres of
> culture.
>
> In this universe, technology also provides the
> great rationalization of the unfreedom of man and
> demonstrates the "technical" impossibility of being
> autonomous, of determining one's own life. For this
> unfreedom appears neither as irrational nor as political,
> but rather as submission to the technical apparatus   ·
> which enlarges the comforts of life and increases the

productivity of labor. Technological rationality thus protects rather than cancels the legitimacy of domination and the instrumentalist horizon of reason opens on a rationally totalitarian society.[6]

Weber's "rationalization" is not only a long-term process of the transformation of social structures but simultaneously "rationalization" in Freud's sense: the true motive, the perpetuation of objectively obsolete domination, is concealed through the invocation of purposive-rational imperatives. This invocation is possible only because the rationality of science and technology is immanently one of control: the rationality of domination.

Marcuse owes this concept, according to which modern science is a historical formation, equally to Husserl's treatise on the crisis of European science and Heidegger's destruction of Western metaphysics. From the materialist position Ernst Bloch has developed the viewpoint that the rationality of modern science is, in its roots, distorted by capitalism in such a way as to rob modern technology of the innocence of a pure productive force. But Marcuse is the first to make the "political content of technical reason" the analytical point of departure for a theory of advanced capitalist society. Because he not only develops this viewpoint philosophically but also attempts to corroborate it through sociological analysis, the difficulties inherent in this conception become visible. I shall refer here to but one ambiguity contained in Marcuse's own conception.

If the phenomenon on which Marcuse bases his social analysis, i.e. the peculiar *fusion of technology and domination*, rationality and oppression, could not be interpreted otherwise than as a world "project," as Marcuse says in the language of Sartre's phenomenology, contained in the material a priori of the logic of science and technology and determined by class interest and historical situation, then social emancipation could not be conceived without a complementary revolutionary transformation of science and technology themselves. In several passages Marcuse is tempted to pursue this idea of a New

Science in connection with the promise, familiar in Jewish and Protestant mysticism, of the "resurrection of fallen nature." This theme, well-known for having penetrated into Schelling's (and Baader's) philosophy via Swabian Pietism, returns in Marx's *Paris Manuscripts*, today constitutes the central thought of Bloch's philosophy, and, in reflected forms, also directs the more secret hopes of Walter Benjamin, Max Horkheimer, and Theodor W. Adorno. It is also present in Marcuse's thought:

> The point which I am trying to make is that science, *by virtue of its own method* and concepts, has projected and promoted a universe in which the domination of nature has remained linked to the domination of man— a link which tends to be fatal to this universe as a whole. Nature, scientifically comprehended and mastered, reappears in the technical apparatus of production and destruction which sustains and improves the life of the individuals while subordinating them to the masters of the apparatus. Thus the rational hierarchy merges with the social one. If this is the case, then the change in the direction of progress, which might sever this fatal link, would also affect the very structure of science—the scientific project. Its hypotheses, without losing their rational character, would develop in an essentially different experimental context (that of a pacified world); consequently, science would arrive at essentially different concepts of nature and establish essentially different facts.[7]

In a logical fashion Marcuse envisages not only different modes of theory formation but a different scientific methodology in general. The transcendental framework within which nature would be made the object of a new experience would then no longer be the functional system of instrumental action. The viewpoint of possible technical control would be replaced by one of preserving, fostering, and releasing the potentialities of nature: "there are two kinds of mastery: a repressive and a liberating one."[8] To this view it must be objected that modern science can be interpreted as a historically unique project only if at least one alternative project is thinkable. And, in addition, an alternative New Science would have to include the definition of a New Technology. This is a sobering consideration because technology, if based at all on a project, can only be traced back to a "project" of the human species *as a whole*, and not to one that could be historically surpassed.

Arnold Gehlen has pointed out in what seems to me conclusive fashion that there is an immanent connection between the technology known to us and the structure of purposive-rational action. If we comprehend the behavioral system of action regulated by its own results as the conjunction of rational decision and instrumental action, then we can reconstruct the history of technology from the point of view of the step-by-step objectivation of the elements of that very system. In any case technological development lends itself to being interpreted as though the human species had taken the elementary components of the behavioral system of purposive-rational action, which is primarily rooted in the human organism, and projected them one after another onto the plane of technical instruments, thereby unburdening itself of the corresponding functions.[9] At first the functions of the motor apparatus (hands and legs) were augmented and replaced, followed by energy production (of the human body), the functions of the sensory apparatus (eyes, ears, and skin), and finally by the functions of the governing center (the brain). Technological development thus follows a logic that corresponds to the structure of purposive-rational action regulated by its own results, which is in fact the structure of *work*. Realizing this, it is impossible to envisage how, as long as the organization of human nature does not change and as long therefore as we have to achieve self-preservation through social labor and with the aid of means that substitute for work, we could renounce technology, more particularly *our* technology, in favor of a qualitatively different one.

Marcuse has in mind an alternative *attitude* to nature,

but it does not admit of the idea of a New Technology. Instead of treating nature as the object of possible technical control, we can encounter her as an opposing partner in a possible interaction. We can seek out a fraternal rather than an exploited nature. At the level of an as yet incomplete intersubjectivity we can impute subjectivity to animals and plants, even to minerals, and try to communicate with nature instead of merely processing her under conditions of severed communication. And the idea that a still enchained subjectivity of nature cannot be unbound until men's communication among themselves is free from domination has retained, to say the least, a singular attraction. Only if men could communicate without compulsion and each could recognize himself in the other, could mankind possibly recognize nature as another subject: not, as idealism would have it, as its Other, but as a subject of which mankind itself is the Other.

Be that as it may, the achievements of technology, which are indispensable as such, could surely not be substituted for by an awakened nature. The alternative to existing technology, the project of nature as opposing partner instead of object, refers to an alternative structure of action: to symbolic interaction in distinction to purposive-rational action. This means, however, that the two projects are projections of work and of language, i.e. projects of the human species as a whole, and not of an individual epoch, a specific class, or a surpassable situation. The idea of a New Science will not stand up to logical scrutiny any more than that of a New Technology, if indeed science is to retain the meaning of modern science inherently oriented to possible technical control. For this function, as for scientific-technical progress in general, there is no more "humane" substitute.

Marcuse himself seems to doubt whether it is meaningful to relativize as a "project" the rationality of science and technology. In many passages of *One-Dimensional Man*, revolutionizing technological rationality means only a transformation of the institutional framework which would leave untouched the forces of production as such. The structure of scientific-technical progress would be conserved, and only the governing values would be changed. New values would be translated into technically solvable tasks. The *direction* of this progress would be new, but the standard of rationality itself would remain unchanged:

> Technics, as a universe of instrumentalities, may
> increase the weakness as well as the power of man.
> At the present stage, he is perhaps more powerless
> over his own apparatus than he ever was before.[10]

This sentence reinstates the political innocence of the forces of production. Here Marcuse is only renewing the classical definition of the relationship between the productive forces and the production relations. But in so doing, he is as far from coming to grips with the new constellation at which he is aiming as he was with the assertion that the productive forces are thoroughly corrupted in their political implications. What is singular about the "rationality" of science and technology is that it characterizes the growing potential of self-surpassing productive forces which continually threaten the institutional framework *and at the same time,* set the standard of legitimation for the production relations that restrict this potential. The dichotomy of this rationality cannot be adequately represented either by historicizing the concept or by returning to the orthodox view: neither the model of the original sin of scientific-technical progress nor that of its innocence do it justice. The most sensible formulation of the matter in question seems to me to be the following:

> The technological *a priori* is a political *a priori*
> inasmuch as the transformation of nature involves
> that of man, and inasmuch as the "man-made
> creations" issue from and reenter a societal ensemble.
> One may still insist that the machinery of the
> technological universe is "as such" indifferent towards
> political ends—it can revolutionize or retard a society.
> An electronic computer can serve equally in capitalist
> or socialist administrations; a cyclotron can be an

> equally efficient tool for a war party or a peace
> party. . . . However, when technics becomes the
> universal form of material production, it circumscribes
> an entire culture; it projects a historical totality—
> a "world."[11]

The difficulty, which Marcuse has only obscured with the notion of the political content of technical reason, is to determine in a categorially precise manner the meaning of the expansion of the rational form of science and technology, i.e. the rationality embodied in systems of purposive-rational action, to the proportions of a life form, of the "historical totality" of a life-world. This is the same process that Weber meant to designate and explain as the rationalization of society. I believe that neither Weber nor Marcuse has satisfactorily accounted for it. Therefore I should like to attempt to reformulate Weber's concept of rationalization in another frame of reference in order to discuss on this new basis Marcuse's critique of Weber, as well as his thesis of the double function of scientific-technical progress (as productive force and as ideology). I am proposing an interpretative scheme that, in the format of an essay, can be introduced but not seriously validated with regard to its utility. The historical generalizations thus serve only to clarify this scheme and are no substitute for its scientific substantiation.

By means of the concept of "rationalization" Weber attempted to grasp the repercussions of scientific-technical progress on the institutional framework of societies engaged in "modernization." He shared this interest with the classical sociological tradition in general, whose pairs of polar concepts all revolve about the same problem: how to construct a conceptual model of the institutional change brought about by the extension of subsystems of purposive-rational action. Status and contract, *Gemeinschaft* and *Gesellschaft*, mechanical and organic solidarity, informal and formal groups, primary and secondary groups, culture and civilization, traditional and bureaucratic authority, sacral and secular associations, military and industrial

society, status group and class—all of these pairs of concepts
represent as many attempts to grasp the structural change of the
institutional framework of a traditional society on the way to
becoming a modern one. Even Parsons' catalog of possible
alternatives of value-orientations belongs in the list of these attempts, although he would not admit it. Parsons claims that his
list systematically represents the decisions between alternative
value-orientations that must be made by the subject of any
action whatsoever, regardless of the particular or historical context. But if one examines the list, one can scarcely overlook the
historical situation of the inquiry on which it is based. The four
pairs of alternative value-orientations,

>*affectivity* versus *affective neutrality*,
>*particularism* versus *universalism*,
>*ascription* versus *achievement*,
>*diffuseness* versus *specificity*,

which are supposed to take into account *all* possible fundamental decisions, are tailored to an analysis of *one* historical
process. In fact they define the relative dimensions of the modification of dominant attitudes in the transition from traditional
to modern society. Subsystems of purposive-rational action do
indeed demand orientation to the postponement of gratification,
universal norms, individual achievement and active mastery,
and specific and analytic relationships, rather than to the opposite orientations.

In order to reformulate what Weber called "rationalization," I should like to go beyond the subjective approach that
Parsons shares with Weber and propose another categorial
framework. I shall take as my starting point the fundamental
distinction between *work* and *interaction*.[12]

By "work" or *purposive-rational action* I understand
either instrumental action or rational choice or their conjunction. Instrumental action is governed by *technical rules* based

on empirical knowledge. In every case they imply conditional predictions about observable events, physical or social. These predictions can prove correct or incorrect. The conduct of rational choice is governed by *strategies* based on analytic knowledge. They imply deductions from preference rules (value systems) and decision procedures; these propositions are either correctly or incorrectly deduced. Purposive-rational action realizes defined goals under given conditions. But while instrumental action organizes means that are appropriate or inappropriate according to criteria of an effective control of reality, strategic action depends only on the correct evaluation of possible alternative choices, which results from calculation supplemented by values and maxims.

By "interaction," on the other hand, I understand *communicative action*, symbolic interaction. It is governed by binding *consensual norms*, which define reciprocal expectations about behavior and which must be understood and recognized by at least two acting subjects. Social norms are enforced through sanctions. Their meaning is objectified in ordinary language communication. While the validity of technical rules and strategies depends on that of empirically true or analytically correct propositions, the validity of social norms is grounded only in the intersubjectivity of the mutual understanding of intentions and secured by the general recognition of obligations. Violation of a rule has a different consequence according to type. *Incompetent* behavior, which violates valid technical rules or strategies, is condemned per se to failure through lack of success; the "punishment" is built, so to speak, into its rebuff by reality. *Deviant* behavior, which violates consensual norms, provokes sanctions that are connected with the rules only externally, that is by convention. Learned rules of purposive-rational action supply us with *skills*, internalized norms with *personality structures*. Skills put us in a position to solve problems; motivations allow us to follow norms. The diagram below summarizes these definitions. They demand a more precise explanation, which I cannot give here. It is above all the bottom column which I am neglecting here, and it refers to the very problem for whose solution I am introducing the distinction between work and interaction.

	Institutional framework: symbolic interaction	Systems of purposive-rational (instrumental and strategic) action
action-orienting rules	social norms	technical rules
level of definition	intersubjectively shared ordinary language	context-free language
type of definition	reciprocal expectations about behavior	conditional predictions conditional imperatives
mechanisms of acquisition	role internalization	learning of skills and qualifications
function of action type	maintenance of institutions (conformity to norms on the basis of reciprocal enforcement)	problem-solving (goal attainment, defined in means-ends relations)
sanctions against violation of rules	punishment on the basis of conventional sanctions: failure against authority	inefficacy: failure in reality
"rationalization"	emancipation, individuation; extension of communication free of domination	growth of productive forces; extension of power of technical control

In terms of the two types of action we can distinguish between social systems according to whether purposive-rational action or interaction predominates. The institutional framework of a society consists of norms that guide symbolic interaction. But there are subsystems such as (to keep to Weber's examples) the economic system or the state apparatus, in which primarily sets of purposive-rational action are institutionalized. These contrast with subsystems such as family and kinship structures, which, although linked to a number of tasks and skills, are primarily based on moral rules of interaction. So I shall distinguish generally at the analytic level between (1) the *institutional framework* of a society or the sociocultural life-world and (2) the *subsystems of purposive-rational action* that are "embedded" in it. Insofar as actions are determined by the institutional framework they are both guided and enforced by norms. Insofar as they are determined by subsystems of purposive-rational action, they conform to patterns of instrumental or strategic action. Of course, only institutionalization can guarantee that such action will in fact follow definite technical rules and expected strategies with adequate probability.

With the help of these distinctions we can reformulate Weber's concept of "rationalization."

The term "traditional society" has come to denote all social systems that generally meet the criteria of civilizations. The latter represent a specific stage in the evolution of the human species. They differ in several traits from more primitive social forms: (1) A centralized ruling power (state organization of political power in contrast to tribal organization); (2) The division of society into socioeconomic classes (distribution to individuals of social obligations and rewards according to class membership and not according to kinship status); (3) The prevalence of a central worldview (myth, complex religion) to the end of legitimating political power (thus converting power into authority). Civilizations are established on the basis of a relatively developed technology and of division of labor in the social process of production, which make possible a surplus product, i.e. a quantity of goods exceeding that needed for the satisfaction of immediate and elementary needs. They owe their existence to the solution of the problem that first arises with the production of a surplus product, namely, how to distribute wealth and labor both unequally and yet legitimately according to criteria other than those generated by a kinship system.[13]

In our context it is relevant that despite considerable differences in their level of development, civilizations, based on an economy dependent on agriculture and craft production, have tolerated technical innovation and organizational improvement only within definite limits. One indicator of the traditional limits to the development of the forces of production is that until about three hundred years ago no major social system had produced more than the equivalent of a maximum of two hundred dollars per capita per annum. The stable pattern of a precapitalist mode of production, preindustrial technology, and premodern science makes possible a typical relation of the institutional framework to subsystems of purposive-rational action. For despite considerable progress, these subsystems, developing out of the system of social labor and its stock of accumulated technically exploitable knowledge, never reached that measure of extension after which their "rationality" would have become an open threat to the authority of the cultural traditions that legitimate political power. The expression "traditional society" refers to the circumstance that the institutional framework is grounded in the unquestionable underpinning of legitimation constituted by mythical, religious or metaphysical interpretations of reality—cosmic as well as social—as a whole. "Traditional" societies exist as long as the development of subsystems of purposive-rational action keep within the limits of the legitimating efficacy of cultural traditions.[14] This is the basis for the "superiority" of the institutional framework, which does not preclude structural changes adapted to a potential surplus generated in the economic system but does preclude critically challenging the traditional form of legitimation. This immunity is a meaningful criterion for the delimitation of traditional societies from those which have crossed the threshold to modernization.

The "superiority criterion," consequently, is applicable to all forms of class society organized as a state in which principles of universally valid rationality (whether of technical or strategic means-ends relations) have not explicitly and successfully called into question the cultural validity of intersubjectively shared traditions, which function as legitimations of the political system. It is only since the capitalist mode of production has equipped the economic system with a self-propelling mechanism that ensures long-term continuous growth (despite crises) in the productivity of labor that the introduction of new technologies and strategies, i.e. innovation as such, has been institutionalized. As Marx and Schumpeter have proposed in their respective theories, the capitalist mode of production can be comprehended as a mechanism that guarantees the *permanent* expansion of subsystems of purposive-rational action and thereby overturns the traditionalist "superiority" of the institutional framework to the forces of production. Capitalism is the first mode of production in world history to institutionalize self-sustaining economic growth. It has generated an industrial system that could be freed from the institutional framework of capitalism and connected to mechanisms other than that of the utilization of capital in private form.

What characterizes the passage from traditional society to society commencing the process of modernization is *not* that structural modification of the institutional framework is necessitated under the pressure of relatively developed productive forces, for that is the mechanism of the evolution of the species from the very beginning. What is new is a level of development of the productive forces that makes permanent the extension of subsystems of purposive-rational action and thereby calls into question the traditional form of the legitimation of power. The older mythic, religious, and metaphysical worldviews obey the logic of interaction contexts. They answer the central questions of men's collective existence and of individual life history. Their themes are justice and freedom, violence and oppression, happiness and gratification, poverty, illness, and death. Their categories are victory and defeat, love and hate, salvation and damnation. Their logic accords with the grammar of systematically distorted communication and with the fateful causality of dissociated symbols and suppressed motives.[15] The rationality of language games, associated with communicative action, is confronted at the threshold of the modern period with the rationality of means-ends relations, associated with instrumental and strategic action. As soon as this confrontation can arise, the end of traditional society is in sight: the traditional form of legitimation breaks down.

Capitalism is defined by a mode of production that not only poses this problem but also solves it. It provides a legitimation of domination which is no longer called down from the lofty heights of cultural tradition but instead summoned up from the base of social labor. The institution of the market, in which private property owners exchange commodities—including the market on which propertyless private individuals exchange their labor power as their only commodity—promises that exchange relations will be and are just owing to equivalence. Even this bourgeois ideology of justice, by adopting the category of reciprocity, still employs a relation of communicative action as the basis of legitimation. But the principle of reciprocity is now the organizing principle of the sphere of production and reproduction itself. Thus on the base of a market economy, political domination can be legitimated henceforth "from below" rather than "from above" (through invocation of cultural tradition).

If we suppose that the division of society into socio-economic classes derives from the differential distribution among social groups of the relevant means of production, and that this distribution itself is based on the institutionalization of relations of social force, then we may assume that in all civilizations this institutional framework has been identical with the system of political domination: traditional authority was political authority. Only with the emergence of the capitalist mode of production can the legitimation of the institutional framework be linked immediately with the system of social labor. Only then can the property order change from a *political relation* to a *production relation*, because it legitimates itself through the rationality of the market, the ideology of exchange society, and no longer through a legitimate power structure. It is now the political system which is justified in terms of the legitimate relations of production: this is the real meaning and function of rationalist natural law from Locke to Kant.[16] The institutional framework of society is only mediately political and immediately economic (the bourgeois constitutional state as "superstructure").

The superiority of the capitalist mode of production to its predecessors has these two roots: the establishment of an economic mechanism that renders permanent the expansion of subsystems of purposive-rational action, and the creation of an economic legitimation by means of which the political system can be adapted to the new requisites of rationality brought about by these developing subsystems. It is this process of adaptation that Weber comprehends as "rationalization." Within it we can distinguish between two tendencies: rationalization "from below" and rationalization "from above."

A permanent pressure for adaptation arises from below as soon as the new mode of production becomes fully operative through the institutionalization of a domestic market for goods and labor power and of the capitalist enterprise. In the system of social labor this institutionalization ensures cumulative progress in the forces of production and an ensuing horizontal extension of subsystems of purposive-rational action—at the cost of economic crises, to be sure. In this way traditional structures are increasingly subordinated to conditions of instrumental or strategic rationality: the organization of labor and of trade, the network of transportation, information, and communication, the institutions of private law, and, starting with financial administration, the state bureaucracy. Thus arises the substructure of a society under the compulsion of modernization. The latter eventually widens to take in all areas of life: the army, the school system, health services, and even the family. Whether in city or country, it induces an urbanization of the *form* of life. That is, it generates subcultures that train the individual to be able to "switch over" at any moment from an interaction context to purposive-rational action.

This pressure for rationalization coming from below is met by a compulsion to rationalize coming from above. For, measured against the new standards of purposive rationality, the power-legitimating and action-orienting traditions—especially mythological interpretations and religious worldviews—lose their cogency. On this level of generalization, what Weber termed "secularization" has two aspects. First, traditional worldviews and objectivations lose their power and validity *as* myth, *as* public religion, *as* customary ritual, *as* justifying metaphysics, *as* unquestionable tradition. Instead, they are reshaped into subjective belief systems and ethics which ensure the private cogency of modern value-orientations (the "Protestant ethic"). Second, they are transformed into constructions that do both at once: criticize tradition and reorganize the released material of tradition according to the principles of formal law and the exchange of equivalents (rationalist natural law). Having become fragile, existing legitimations are replaced by new ones. The latter emerge from the critique of the dogmatism of traditional interpretations of the world and claim a scientific character. Yet they retain legitimating functions, thereby keeping actual power relations inaccessible to analysis and to public consciousness. It is in this way that ideologies in the restricted sense first came into being. They replace traditional legitimations of power by appearing in the mantle of modern science and by deriving their justification from the critique of ideology. Ideologies are coeval with the critique of ideology. In this sense there can be no prebourgeois "ideologies."

In this connection modern science assumes a singular function. In distinction from the philosophical sciences of the older sort, the empirical sciences have developed since Galileo's time within a methodological frame of reference that reflects the transcendental viewpoint of possible technical control. Hence the modern sciences produce knowledge which through its *form* (and not through the subjective intention of scientists) is technically exploitable knowledge, although the possible applications generally are realized afterwards. Science and technology were not interdependent until late into the nineteenth century. Until then modern science did not contribute to the acceleration of technical development nor, consequently, to the pressure toward rationalization from below. Rather, its contribution to the modernization process was indirect. Modern physics gave rise to a philosophical approach that interpreted nature and society according to a model borrowed from the natural sciences and induced, so to speak, the mechanistic worldview of the seventeenth century. The reconstruction of classical natural law was carried out in this framework. This modern natural law was the basis of the bourgeois revolutions of the seventeenth, eighteenth, and nineteenth centuries, through which the old legitimations of the power structure were finally destroyed.[17]

By the middle of the nineteenth century the capitalist mode of production had developed so fully in England and France that Marx was able to identify the locus of the institutional framework of society in the relations of production and at the same time criticize the legitimating basis constituted by the exchange of equivalents. He carried out the critique of bourgeois ideology in the form of *political economy*. His labor theory of value destroyed the semblance of freedom, by means of which the legal institution of the free labor contract had made unrecognizable the relationship of social force that underlay the wage-labor relationship. Marcuse's criticism of Weber is that the latter, disregarding this Marxian insight, upholds an abstract concept of rationalization, which not merely fails to express the specific class content of the adaptation of the institutional framework to the developing systems of purposive-rational action, but conceals it. Marcuse knows that the Marxian analysis can no longer be applied as it stands to advanced capitalist society, with which Weber was already confronted. But he wants to show through the example of Weber that the evolution of modern society in the framework of state-regulated capitalism cannot be conceptualized if liberal capitalism has not been analyzed adequately.

Since the last quarter of the nineteenth century two developmental tendencies have become noticeable in the most advanced capitalist countries: an increase in state intervention in order to secure the system's stability, and a growing interdependence of research and technology, which has turned the sciences into the leading productive force. Both tendencies have destroyed the particular constellation of institutional framework and subsystems of purposive-rational action which characterized liberal capitalism, thereby eliminating the conditions relevant for the application of political economy in the version correctly formulated by Marx for liberal capitalism. I believe that Marcuse's basic thesis, according to which technology and science today also take on the function of legitimating political power, is the key to analyzing the changed constellation.

The permanent regulation of the economic process by means of state intervention arose as a defense mechanism against the dysfunctional tendencies, which threaten the system, that capitalism generates when left to itself. Capitalism's actual development manifestly contradicted the capitalist idea of a bourgeois society, emancipated from domination, in which power is neutralized. The root ideology of just exchange, which Marx unmasked in theory, collapsed in practice. The form of capital utilization through private ownership could only be maintained by the governmental corrective of a social and economic policy that stabilized the business cycle. The institutional framework of society was repoliticized. It no longer coincides immediately with the relations of production, i.e. with an order of private law that secures capitalist economic activity and the corresponding general guarantees of order provided by the bourgeois state. But this means a change in the relation of the economy to the political system: politics is no longer *only* a phenomenon of the superstructure. If society no longer "autonomously" perpetuates itself through self-regulation as a sphere preceding and lying at the basis of the state—and its ability to do so was the really novel feature of the capitalist mode of production—then society and the state are no longer in the relationship that Marxian theory had defined as that of base and superstructure. Then, however, a critical theory of society can no longer be constructed in the exclusive form of a critique of political economy. A point of view that methodically isolates the economic laws of motion of society can claim to grasp the overall structure of social life in its essential categories only as long as politics depends on the economic base. It becomes inapplicable when the "base" has to be comprehended as in itself a function of governmental activity and political conflicts. According to Marx, the critique of political economy was the theory of bourgeois society only as *critique of ideology*. If, however, the ideology of just exchange disintegrates, then the power structure can no longer be criticized *immediately* at the level of the relations of production.

With the collapse of this ideology, political power requires a new legitimation. Now since the power indirectly exercised over the exchange process is itself operating under political
control and state regulation, legitimation can no longer be
derived from the unpolitical order constituted by the relations
of production. To this extent the requirement for direct legitimation, which exists in precapitalist societies, reappears. On the
other hand, the resuscitation of immediate political domination
(in the traditional form of legitimation on the basis of cosmo-
logical worldviews) has become impossible. For traditions
have already been disempowered. Moreover, in industrially
developed societies the results of bourgeois emancipation from
immediate political domination (civil and political rights and the
mechanism of general elections) can be fully ignored only in
periods of reaction. Formally democratic government in systems of state-regulated capitalism is subject to a need for legitimation which cannot be met by a return to a prebourgeois
form. Hence the ideology of free exchange is replaced by a
substitute program. The latter is oriented not to the social
results of the institution of the market but to those of government action designed to compensate for the dysfunctions of
free exchange. This policy combines the element of the bourgeois ideology of achievement (which, however, displaces assignment of status according to the standard of individual
achievement from the market to the school system) with a
guaranteed minimum level of welfare, which offers secure employment and a stable income. This substitute program obliges
the political system to maintain stabilizing conditions for an
economy that guards against risks to growth and guarantees
social security and the chance for individual upward mobility.
What is needed to this end is latitude for manipulation by state
interventions that, at the cost of limiting the institutions of
private law, secure the private form of capital utilization *and
bind the masses' loyalty to this form.*

Insofar as government action is directed toward the
economic system's stability and growth, politics now takes on
a peculiarly negative character. For it is oriented toward the
elimination of dysfunctions and the avoidance of risks that

threaten the system: not, in other words, toward the *realization of practical goals* but toward the *solution of technical problems.* Claus Offe pointed this out in his paper at the 1968 Frankfurt Sociological Conference:

> In this structure of the relation of economy and the state, "politics" degenerates into action that follows numerous and continually emerging "avoidance imperatives": the mass of differentiated social-scientific information that flows into the political system allows both the early identification of risk zones and the treatment of actual dangers. What is new about this structure is . . . that the risks to stability built into the mechanism of private capital utilization in highly organized markets, risks that can be manipulated, prescribe preventive actions and measures that *must* be accepted as long as they are to accord with the existing legitimation resources (i.e., substitute program).[18]

Offe perceives that through these preventive action-orientations, government activity is restricted to administratively soluble technical problems, so that practical questions evaporate, so to speak. *Practical substance is eliminated.*

Old-style politics was forced, merely through its traditional form of legitimation, to define itself in relation to practical goals: the "good life" was interpreted in a context defined by interaction relations. The same still held for the ideology of bourgeois society. The substitute program prevailing today, in contrast, is aimed exclusively at the functioning of a manipulated system. It eliminates practical questions and therewith precludes discussion about the adoption of standards; the latter could emerge only from a democratic decision-making process. The solution of technical problems is not dependent on public discussion. Rather, public discussions could render problematic the framework within which the tasks of government action present themselves as technical ones. Therefore the new politics of state interventionism requires a depoliticization of the mass of the population. To the extent that practical questions are eliminated, the public realm also loses its political function. At the same time, the institutional framework of society is still distinct from the systems of purposive-rational action themselves. Its organization continues to be a problem of *practice* linked to communication, not one of *technology*, no matter how scientifically guided. Hence, the bracketing out of practice associated with the new kind of politics is not automatic. The substitute program, which legitimates power today, leaves unfilled a vital need for legitimation: how will the depoliticization of the masses be made plausible to them? Marcuse would be able to answer: by having technology and science *also* take on the role of an ideology.

Since the end of the nineteenth century the other developmental tendency characteristic of advanced capitalism has become increasingly momentous: the scientization of technology. The institutional pressure to augment the productivity of labor through the introduction of new technology has always existed under capitalism. But innovations depended on sporadic inventions, which, while economically motivated, were still fortuitous in character. This changed as technical development entered into a feedback relation with the progress of the modern sciences. With the advent of large-scale industrial research, science, technology, and industrial utilization were fused into a system. Since then, industrial research has been linked up with research under government contract, which primarily promotes scientific and technical progress in the military sector. From there information flows back into the sectors of civilian production. Thus technology and science become a leading productive force, rendering inoperative the conditions for Marx's labor theory of value. It is no longer meaningful to calculate the amount of capital investment in research and development on the basis of the value of unskilled (simple) labor power, when scientific-technical progress has become an independent source of surplus value, in relation to which the only source of surplus value considered by Marx, namely the labor power of the immediate producers, plays an ever smaller role.[19]

As long as the productive forces were visibly linked to the rational decisions and instrumental action of men engaged in social production, they could be understood as the potential for a growing power of technical control and not be confused with the institutional framework in which they are embedded. However, with the institutionalization of scientific-technical progress, the potential of the productive forces has assumed a form owing to which men lose consciousness of the dualism of work and interaction.

It is true that social interests still determine the direction, functions, and pace of technical progress. But these interests define the social system so much as a whole that they coincide with the interest in maintaining the system. *As such* the private form of capital utilization and a distribution mechanism for social rewards that guarantees the loyalty of the masses are removed from discussion. The quasi-autonomous progress of science and technology then appears as an independent variable on which the most important single system variable, namely economic growth, depends. Thus arises a perspective in which the development of the social system *seems* to be determined by the logic of scientific-technical progress. The immanent law of this progress seems to produce objective exigencies, which must be obeyed by any politics oriented toward functional needs. But when this semblance has taken root effectively, then propaganda can refer to the role of technology and science in order to explain and legitimate why in modern societies the process of democratic decision-making about practical problems loses its function and "must" be replaced by plebiscitary decisions about alternative sets of leaders of administrative personnel. This technocracy thesis has been worked out in several versions on the intellectual level.[20] What seems to me more important is that it can also become a background ideology that penetrates into the consciousness of the depoliticized mass of the population, where it can take on legitimating power.[21] It is a singular achievement of this ideology to detach society's self-understanding from the frame of reference of communicative action and from the concepts of symbolic interaction and replace it with a scientific model. Accordingly the culturally defined self-understanding of a social life-world is replaced by the self-reification of men under categories of purposive-rational action and adaptive behavior.

The model according to which the planned reconstruction of society is to proceed is taken from systems analysis. It is possible in principle to comprehend and analyze individual enterprises and organizations, even political or economic subsystems and social systems as a whole, according to the pattern of self-regulated systems. It makes a difference, of course, whether we use a cybernetic frame of reference for analytic purposes or *organize* a given social system in accordance with this pattern as a man-machine system. But the transferral of the analytic model to the level of social organization is implied by the very approach taken by systems analysis. Carrying out this intention of an instinct-like self-stabilization of social systems yields the peculiar perspective that the structure of one of the two types of action, namely the behavioral system of purposive-rational action, not only predominates over the institutional framework but gradually absorbs communicative action as such. If, with Arnold Gehlen, one were to see the inner logic of technical development as the step-by-step disconnection of the behavioral system of purposive-rational action from the human organism and its transferral to machines, then the technocratic intention could be understood as the last stage of this development. For the first time man can not only, as *homo faber*, completely objectify himself and confront the achievements that have taken on independent life in his products; he can in addition, as *homo fabricatus*, be integrated into his technical apparatus if the structure of purposive-rational action can be successfully reproduced on the level of social systems. According to this idea the institutional framework of society —which previously was rooted in a different type of action— would now, in a fundamental reversal, be *absorbed* by the subsystems of purposive-rational action, which were embedded in it.

Of course this technocratic intention has not been realized anywhere even in its beginnings. But it serves as an ideology for the new politics, which is adapted to technical problems and brackets out practical questions. Furthermore it does correspond to certain developmental tendencies that could lead to a creeping erosion of what we have called the institutional framework. The manifest domination of the authoritarian state gives way to the manipulative compulsions of technical-operational administration. The moral realization of a normative order is a function of communicative action oriented to shared cultural meaning and presupposing the internalization of values. It is increasingly supplanted by conditioned behavior, while large organizations as such are increasingly patterned after the structure of purposive-rational action. The industrially most advanced societies seem to approximate the model of behavioral control steered by external stimuli rather than guided by norms. Indirect control through fabricated stimuli has increased, especially in areas of putative subjective freedom (such as electoral, consumer, and leisure behavior). Sociopsychologically, the era is typified less by the authoritarian personality than by the de-structuring of the superego. The increase in *adaptive behavior* is, however, only the obverse of the dissolution of the sphere of linguistically mediated interaction by the structure of purposive-rational action. This is paralleled subjectively by the disappearance of the difference between purposive-rational action and interaction from the consciousness not only of the sciences of man, but of men themselves. The concealment of this difference proves the ideological power of the technocratic consciousness.

In consequence of the two tendencies that have been discussed, capitalist society has changed to the point where two key categories of Marxian theory, namely class struggle and ideology, can no longer be employed as they stand.

It was on the basis of the capitalist mode of production that the struggle of social classes as such was first constituted, thereby creating an objective situation from which the class structure of traditional society, with its immediately political constitution, could be *recognized* in retrospect. State-regulated capitalism, which emerged from a reaction against the dangers to the system produced by open class antagonism, suspends class conflict. The system of advanced capitalism is so defined by a policy of securing the loyalty of the wage-earning masses through rewards, that is, by avoiding conflict, that the conflict still built into the structure of society in virtue of the private mode of capital utilization is the very area of conflict which has the greatest probability of remaining latent. It recedes behind others, which, while conditioned by the mode of production, can no longer assume the form of class conflicts. In the paper cited, Claus Offe has analyzed this paradoxical state of affairs, showing that open conflicts about social interests break out with greater probability the less their frustration has dangerous consequences for the system. The needs with the greatest conflict potential are those on the periphery of the area of state intervention. They are far from the central conflict being kept in a state of latency and therefore they are not seen as having priority among dangers to be warded off. Conflicts are set off by these needs to the extent that disproportionately scattered state interventions produce backward areas of development and corresponding disparity tensions:

> The disparity between areas of life grows above all
> in view of the differential state of development
> obtaining between the actually institutionalized and
> the possible level of technical and social progress.
> The disproportion between the most modern
> apparatuses for industrial and military purposes and
> the stagnating organization of the transport, health,
> and educational systems is just as well known an
> example of this disparity between areas of life as is the
> contradiction between rational planning and
> regulation in taxation and finance policy and the
> unplanned, haphazard development of cities and
> regions. Such contradictions can no longer be
> designated accurately as antagonisms between classes,
> yet they can still be interpreted as results of the still
> dominant process of the private utilization of
> capital and of a specifically capitalist power structure.
> In this process the prevailing interests are those which,

without being clearly localizable, are in a position, on the basis of the established mechanism of the capitalist economy, to react to disturbances of the conditions of their stability by producing risks relevant to the system as a whole.[22]

The interests bearing on the maintenance of the mode of production can no longer be "clearly localized" in the social system as class interests. For the power structure, aimed as it is at avoiding dangers to the system, precisely excludes "domination" (as immediate political or economically mediated social force) exercised in such a manner that one class subject *confronts* another as an identifiable group.

This means not that class antagonisms have been abolished but that they have become *latent*. Class distinctions persist in the form of subcultural traditions and corresponding differences not only in the standard of living and life style but also in political attitude. The social structure also makes it probable that the class of wage earners will be hit harder than other groups by social disparities. And finally, the generalized interest in perpetuating the system is still anchored today, on the level of immediate life chances, in a structure of privilege. The concept of an interest that has become *completely* independent of living subjects would cancel itself out. But with the deflection of dangers to the system in state-regulated capitalism, the political system has incorporated an interest—which transcends latent class boundaries—in preserving the compensatory distribution façade.

Furthermore, the displacement of the conflict zone from the class boundary to the underprivileged regions of life does not mean at all that serious conflict potential has been disposed of. As the extreme example of racial conflict in the United States shows, so many consequences of disparity can accumulate in certain areas and groups that explosions resembling civil war can occur. But unless they are connected with protest potential from other sectors of society no conflicts arising from such underprivilege can really overturn the system —they can only provoke it to sharp reactions incompatible with formal democracy. For underprivileged groups are not social classes, nor do they ever even potentially represent the mass of the population. Their *disfranchisement* and pauperization no longer coincide with *exploitation,* because the system does not live off their labor. They can represent at most a past phase of exploitation. But they cannot through the withdrawal of cooperation attain the demands that they legitimately put forward. That is why these demands retain an appellative character. In the case of long-term nonconsideration of their legitimate demands underprivileged groups can in extreme situations react with desperate destruction and self-destruction. But as long as no coalitions are made with privileged groups, such a civil war lacks the chance of revolutionary success that class struggle possesses.

With a series of restrictions this model seems applicable even to the relations between the industrially advanced nations and the formerly colonial areas of the Third World. Here, too, growing disparity leads to a form of underprivilege that in the future surely will be increasingly less comprehensible through categories of exploitation. Economic interests are replaced on this level, however, with immediately military ones.

Be that as it may, in advanced capitalist society deprived and privileged groups no longer confront each other *as* socio-economic classes—and to some extent the boundaries of under-privilege are no longer even specific to groups and instead run across population categories. Thus the fundamental relation that existed in all traditional societies and that came to the fore under liberal capitalism is mediatized, namely the class antagonism between partners who stand in an institutionalized relationship of force, economic exploitation, and political oppression to one another, and in which communication is so distorted and restricted that the legitimations serving as an ideological veil cannot be called into question. Hegel's concept of the ethical totality of a living relationship which is sundered because one subject does not reciprocally satisfy the needs of the other is no longer an appropriate model for the mediatized class structure of organized, advanced capitalism. The suspended dialectic of the ethical generates the peculiar semblance of *post-histoire.* The reason is that relative growth of the productive forces no longer represents *eo ipso* a potential that points beyond the existing framework with emancipatory consequences, in view of which legitimations of an existing power structure become enfeebled. For the leading productive force—controlled scientific-technical progress itself—has now become the basis of legitimation. Yet this new form of legitimation has cast off the old shape of *ideology*.

Technocratic consciousness is, on the one hand, "less ideological" than all previous ideologies. For it does not have the opaque force of a delusion that only transfigures the implementation of interests. On the other hand today's dominant, rather glassy background ideology, which makes a fetish of science, is more irresistible and farther-reaching than ideologies of the old type. For with the veiling of practical problems it not only justifies a *particular class's* interest in domination and represses *another class's* partial need for emancipation, but affects the human race's emancipatory interest as such.

Technocratic consciousness is not a rationalized, wish-fulfilling fantasy, not an "illusion" in Freud's sense, in which a system of interaction is either represented or interpreted and grounded. Even bourgeois ideologies could be traced back to a basic pattern of just interactions, free of domination and mutually satisfactory. It was these ideologies which met the criteria of wish-fulfillment and substitute gratification; the communication on which they were based was so limited by repressions that the relation of force once institutionalized as the capital-labor relation could not even be called by name. But the technocratic consciousness is not based in the same way on the causality of dissociated symbols and unconscious motives, which generates both false consciousness and the power of reflection to which the critique of ideology is indebted. It is less vulnerable to reflection, because it is no longer *only* ideology. For it does not, in the manner of ideology, express a projection of the "good life" (which even if not identifiable with a bad reality, can at least be brought into virtually satisfactory accord with it). Of course the new ideology, like the old, serves to impede making the foundations of society the object of thought and reflection. Previously, social force lay at the basis of the relation between capitalist and wage-laborers. Today the basis is provided by structural conditions which predefine the tasks of system maintenance: the private form of capital utilization and a political form of distributing social rewards that guarantees mass loyalty. However, the old and new ideology differ in two ways.

First, the capital-labor relation today, because of its linkage to a loyalty-ensuring political distribution mechanism, no longer engenders uncorrected exploitation and oppression. The process through which the persisting class antagonism has been made virtual presupposes that the repression on which the latter is based first came to consciousness in history and *only then* was stabilized in a modified form as a property of the system. Technocratic consciousness, therefore, cannot rest in the same way on collective repression as did earlier ideologies. Second, mass loyalty today is created only with the aid of rewards for *privatized needs*. The achievements in virtue of which the system justifies itself may not in principle be interpreted politically. The acceptable interpretation is immediately in terms of allocations of money and leisure time (neutral with regard to their use), and mediately in terms of the technocratic justification of the occlusion of practical questions. Hence the new ideology is distinguished from its predecessor in that it severs the criteria for justifying the organization of social life from any normative regulation of interaction, thus depoliticizing them. It anchors them instead in functions of a putative system of purposive-rational action.

Technocratic consciousness reflects not the sundering of an ethical situation but the repression of "ethics" as such as a category of life. The common, positivist way of thinking renders inert the frame of reference of interaction in ordinary language, in which domination and ideology both arise under conditions of distorted communication and can be reflectively detected and broken down. The depoliticization of the mass of the population, which is legitimated through technocratic consciousness, is at the same time men's self-objectification in categories equally of both purposive-rational action and adaptive behavior. The reified models of the sciences migrate into the sociocultural life-world and gain objective power over the latter's self-understanding. The ideological nucleus of this consciousness is *the elimination of the distinction between the practical and the technical*. It reflects, but does not objectively account for, the new constellation of a disempowered institutional framework and systems of purposive-rational action that have taken on a life of their own.

The new ideology consequently violates an interest grounded in one of the two fundamental conditions of our cultural existence: in language, or more precisely, in the form of socialization and individuation determined by communication in ordinary language. This interest extends to the maintenance of intersubjectivity of mutual understanding as well as to the creation of communication without domination. Technocratic consciousness makes this practical interest disappear behind the interest in the expansion of our power of technical control. Thus the reflection that the new ideology calls for must penetrate beyond the level of particular historical class interests to disclose the fundamental interests of mankind as such, engaged in the process of self-constitution.[23]

If the relativization of the field of application of the concept of ideology and the theory of class be confirmed, then the category framework developed by Marx in the basic assumptions of historical materialism requires a new formulation. The model of forces of production and relations of production would have to be replaced by the more abstract one of work and interaction. The relations of production designate a level on which the institutional framework was anchored only during the phase of the development of liberal capitalism, and not either before or after. To be sure, the productive forces, in which the learning processes organized in the subsystems of purposive-rational action accumulate, have been from the very beginning the motive force of social evolution. But, they do not appear, as Marx supposed, *under all circumstances* to be a po-

tential for liberation and to set off emancipatory movements—
at least not once the continual growth of the productive forces
has become dependent on scientific-technical progress that has
also taken on functions of *legitimating political power*. I suspect
that the frame of reference developed in terms of the analogous,
but more general relation of institutional framework (interaction) and subsystems of purposive-rational action ("work" in
the broad sense of instrumental and strategic action) is more
suited to reconstructing the sociocultural phases of the history
of mankind.

There are several indications that during the long initial
phase until the end of the Mesolithic period, purposive-rational
actions could only be motivated at all through ritual attachment
to interactions. A profane realm of subsystems of purposive-
rational action seems to have separated out from the institutional
framework of symbolic interaction in the first settled cultures,
based on the domestication of animals and cultivation of plants.
But it was probably only in civilizations, that is under the
conditions of a class society organized as a state that the differentiation of work and interaction went far enough for the subsystems to yield technically exploitable knowledge that could
be stored and expanded relatively independently of mythical
and religious interpretations of the world. At the same time social norms became separated from power-legitimating traditions,
so that "culture" attained a certain independence from "institutions." The threshold of the modern period would then be
characterized by that process of rationalization which com-
menced with loss of the "superiority" of the institutional framework to the subsystems of purposive-rational action. Traditional
legitimations could now be criticized against the standards of
rationality of means-ends relations. Concurrently, information
from the area of technically exploitable knowledge infiltrated
tradition and compelled a reconstruction of traditional world
interpretations along the lines of scientific standards.

We have followed this process of "rationalization from
above" up to the point where technology and science themselves
in the form of a common positivistic way of thinking, articulated as technocratic consciousness, began to take the role of a

substitute ideology for the demolished bourgeois ideologies. This point was reached with the critique of bourgeois ideologies. It introduced ambiguity into the concept of rationalization. This ambiguity was deciphered by Horkheimer and Adorno as the dialectic of enlightenment, which has been refined by Marcuse as the thesis that technology and science themselves become ideological.

From the very beginning the pattern of human sociocultural development has been determined by a growing power of technical control over the external conditions of existence on the one hand, and a more or less passive adaptation of the institutional framework to the expanded subsystems of purposive-rational action on the other. Purposive-rational action represents the form of *active* adaptation, which distinguishes the collective *self*-preservation of societal subjects from the preservation of the species characteristic of other animals. We know how to bring the relevant conditions of life under control, that is, we know how to adapt the environment to our needs culturally rather than adapting ourselves to external nature. In contrast, changes of the institutional framework, to the extent that they are derived immediately or mediately from new technologies or improved strategies (in the areas of production, transportation, weaponry, etc.) have not taken the same form of active adaptation. In general such modifications follow the pattern of *passive* adaptation. They are not the result of planned purposive-rational action geared to its own consequences, but the product of fortuitous, undirected development. Yet it was impossible to become conscious of this disproportion between active and passive adaptation as long as the dynamics of capitalist development remained concealed by bourgeois ideologies. Only with the critique of bourgeois ideologies did this disproportion enter public consciousness.

The most impressive witness to this experience is still the *Communist Manifesto*. In rapturous words Marx eulogizes the revolutionary role of the bourgeoisie:

> The bourgeoisie cannot exist without constantly revolutionizing the instruments of production, and

thereby the relations of production, and with them
the whole relations of society.

In another passage he writes:

> The bourgeoisie, during its rule of scarce one
> hundred years, has created more massive and more
> colossal productive forces than have all preceding
> generations together. Subjection of nature's forces
> to man, machinery, application of chemistry to
> industry and agriculture, steam navigation, railways,
> electric telegraphs, clearing of whole continents for
> cultivation, canalization of rivers, whole populations
> conjured out of the ground . . .

Marx also perceives the reaction of this development back upon
the institutional framework:

> All fixed, fast-frozen relations, with their train of
> ancient and venerable prejudices and opinions, are
> swept away, all new-formed ones become antiquated
> before they can ossify. All that is solid melts into air,
> all that is holy is profaned, and man is at last compelled
> to face with sober senses his real conditions of life
> and his relations with his kind.

It is with regard to the disproportion between the passive adaptation of the institutional framework and the "active
subjection of nature" that the assertion that men make their
history, but not with 'will or consciousness, was formulated. It
was the aim of Marx's critique to transform the secondary
adaptation of the institutional framework as well into an active
one, and to bring under control the structural change of society
itself. This would overcome a fundamental condition of all
previous history and complete the self-constitution of mankind:
the end of prehistory. But this idea was ambiguous.

Marx, to be sure, viewed the problem of making history

with will and consciousness as one of the *practical* mastery of previously ungoverned processes of social development. Others, however, have understood it as a *technical* problem. They want to bring society under control in the same way as nature by reconstructing it according to the pattern of self-regulated systems of purposive-rational action and adaptive behavior. This intention is to be found not only among technocrats of capitalist planning but also among those of bureaucratic socialism. Only the technocratic consciousness obscures the fact that this reconstruction could be achieved at no less a cost than closing off the only dimension that is essential, because it is susceptible to humanization, *as* a structure of interactions mediated by ordinary language. In the future the repertoire of control techniques will be considerably expanded. On Herman Kahn's list of the most probable technical innovations of the next thirty years I observe among the first fifty items a large number of techniques of behavioral and personality change:

> *30.* new and possibly pervasive techniques for surveillance, monitoring and control of individuals and organizations;
> *33.* new and more reliable "educational" and propaganda techniques affecting human behavior— public and private;
> *34.* practical use of direct electronic communication with and stimulation of the brain;
> *37.* new and relatively effective counterinsurgency techniques;
> *39.* new and more varied drugs for control of fatigue, relaxation, alertness, mood, personality, perceptions, and fantasies;
> *41.* improved capability to "change" sex;
> *42.* other genetic control or influence over the basic constitution of an individual.[24]

A prediction of this sort is extremely controversial. Nevertheless, it points to an area of future possibilities of detaching human behavior from a normative system linked to the grammar of language-games and integrating it instead into self-regulated subsystems of the man-machine type by means of immediate physical or psychological control. Today the psychotechnic manipulation of behavior can already liquidate the old fashioned detour through norms that are internalized but capable of reflection. Behavioral control could be instituted at an even deeper level tomorrow through biotechnic intervention in the endocrine regulating system, not to mention the even greater consequences of intervening in the genetic transmission of inherited information. If this occurred, old regions of consciousness developed in ordinary-language communication would of necessity completely dry up. At this stage of human engineering, if the end of psychological manipulation could be spoken of in the same sense as the end of ideology is today, the spontaneous alienation derived from the uncontrolled lag of the institutional framework would be overcome. But the self-objectivation of man would have fulfilled itself in planned alienation —men would make their history with will, but without consciousness.

I am not asserting that this cybernetic dream of the instinct-like self-stabilization of societies is being fulfilled or that it is even realizable. I do think, however, that it follows through certain vague but basic assumptions of technocratic consciousness to their conclusion as a negative utopia and thus denotes an evolutionary trend that is taking shape under the slick domination of technology and science as ideology. Above all, it becomes clear against this background that *two concepts of rationalization* must be distinguished. At the level of subsystems of purposive-rational action, scientific-technical progress has already compelled the reorganization of social institutions and sectors, and necessitates it on an even larger scale than heretofore. But this process of the development of the productive forces can be a potential for liberation if and only if it does not replace rationalization on another level. *Rationalization at the level of the institutional framework* can occur only in the medium of symbolic interaction itself, that is, through *removing restrictions on communication*. Public, unrestricted discussion, free from domination, of the suitability and desirability of action-orienting principles and norms in the light of the socio-cultural repercussions of developing subsystems of purposive-rational action—such communication at all levels of political and repoliticized decision-making processes is the only medium in which anything like "rationalization" is possible.

In such a process of generalized reflection institutions would alter their specific composition, going beyond the limit of a mere change in legitimation. A rationalization of social norms would, in fact, be characterized by a decreasing degree of repressiveness (which at the level of personality structure should increase average tolerance of ambivalence in the face of role conflicts), a decreasing degree of rigidity (which should multiply the chances of an individually stable self-presentation in everyday interactions), and approximation to a type of be-havioral control that would allow role distance and the flexible application of norms that, while well-internalized, would be accessible to reflection. Rationalization measured by changes in these three dimensions does not lead, as does the rationalization of purposive-rational subsystems, to an increase in technical control over objectified processes of nature and society. It does not lead per se to the better functioning of social systems, but would furnish the members of society with the opportunity for further emancipation and progressive individuation. The growth of productive forces is not the same as the intention of the "good life." It can at best serve it.

I do not even think that the model of a technologically possible surplus that cannot be used in full measure within a repressively maintained institutional framework (Marx speaks of "fettered" forces of production) is appropriate to state-regulated capitalism. Today, better utilization of an unrealized potential leads to improvement of the economic-industrial ap-paratus, but no longer *eo ipso* to a transformation of the institu-tional framework with emancipatory consequences. The question is not whether we completely *utilize* an available or creatable potential, but whether we *choose* what we want for the purpose of the pacification and gratification of existence. But it must be immediately noted that we are only posing this question and cannot answer it in advance. For the solution demands precisely that unrestricted communication about the goals of life activity and conduct against which advanced capitalism, structurally dependent on a depoliticized public realm, puts up a strong resistance.

A new conflict zone, in place of the virtualized class antagonism and apart from the disparity conflicts at the margins of the system, can only emerge where advanced capitalist society has to immunize itself, by depoliticizing the masses of the population, against the questioning of its technocratic background ideology: in the public sphere administered through the mass media. For only here is it possible to buttress the concealment of the difference between progress in systems of purposive-rational action and emancipatory transformations of the institutional framework, between technical and practical problems. And it is necessary for the system to conceal this difference. Publicly administered definitions extend to *what* we want for our lives, but not to *how* we would like to live if we could find out, with regard to attainable potentials, how we *could* live.

Who will activate this conflict zone is hard to predict. Neither the old class antagonism nor the new type of underprivilege contains a protest potential whose origins make it tend toward the repoliticization of the desiccated public sphere. For the present, the only protest potential that gravitates toward the new conflict zone owing to identifiable interests is arising among certain groups of university, college, and high school students. Here we can make three observations:

1. Protesting students are a privileged group, which advances no interests that proceed immediately from its social situation or that could be satisfied in conformity with the system through an augmentation of social rewards. The first American studies of student activists conclude that they are predominantly not from upwardly mobile sections of the student body, but rather from sections with privileged status recruited from economically advantaged social strata.[25]

2. For plausible reasons the legitimations offered by the political system do not seem convincing to this group. The welfare-state substitute program for decrepit bourgeois ideol-

ogies presupposes a certain status and achievement orientation. According to the studies cited, student activists are less privatistically oriented to professional careers and future families than other students. Their academic achievements, which tend to be above average, and their social origins do not promote a horizon of expectations determined by anticipated exigencies of the labor market. Active students, who relatively frequently are in the social sciences and humanities, tend to be immune to technocratic consciousness because, although for varying motives, their primary experiences in their own intellectual work in neither case accord with the basic technocratic assumptions.

3. Among this group, conflict cannot break out because of the extent of the discipline and burdens imposed, but only because of their quality. Students are not fighting for a larger share of social rewards in the prevalent categories: income and leisure time. Instead, their protest is directed against the very category of reward itself. The few available data confirm the supposition that the protest of youth from bourgeois homes no longer coincides with the pattern of authority conflict typical of previous generations. Student activists tend to have parents who share their critical attitude. They have been brought up relatively frequently with more psychological understanding and according to more liberal educational principles than comparable inactive groups.[26] Their socialization seems to have been achieved in subcultures freed from immediate economic compulsion, in which the traditions of bourgeois morality and their petit-bourgeois derivatives have lost their function. This means that training for switching over to value-orientations of purposive-rational action no longer includes fetishizing this form of action. These educational techniques make possible experiences and favor orientations that clash with the conserved life form of an economy of poverty. What can take shape on this basis is a lack of understanding in principle for the reproduction of virtues and sacrifices that have become superfluous— a lack of understanding why despite the advanced stage of technological development the life of the individual is still determined by the dictates of professional careers, the ethics of status competition, and by values of possessive individualism

and available substitute gratifications: why the institutionalized struggle for existence, the discipline of alienated labor, and the eradication of sensuality and aesthetic gratification are perpetuated. To this sensibility the structural elimination of practical problems from a depoliticized public realm must become unbearable. However, it will give rise to a political force only if this sensibility comes into contact with a problem that the system cannot solve. For the future I see *one* such problem. The amount of social wealth produced by industrially advanced capitalism and the technical and organizational conditions under which this wealth is produced make it ever more difficult to link status assignment in an even subjectively convincing manner to the mechanism for the evaluation of individual achievement.[27] In the long run therefore, student protest could permanently destroy this crumbling achievement-ideology, and thus bring down the already fragile legitimating basis of advanced capitalism, which rests only on depoliticization.

Notes

Chapter 1   The University in a Democracy

1. See the suggestions for the structure of new universities made by the Council on Education and Culture (*Wissenschaftsrat*) and published in Tübingen in 1962.

2. For issues of university politics within the institution itself, all parties must naturally be granted the opportunity of demonstrating the decisions they have arrived at rationally. The means chosen by students should complement the means of the organization of authority with which they are confronted. This applies with regard to specific goals of university politics that are in principle capable of being realized. In contrast, however, the permanent mobilization of the student body as a self-sufficient activity, independent of such goals, that maintained itself only for the purpose of politicizing consciousness as a Jacobin education process could not be legitimated *on the only basis* being used here to justify politics as an inalienable part of the intrauniversity community. Nevertheless, permanent mobilization of this sort could be rendered comprehensible as a reaction of self-defense in the event of a suspension of public discourse on the intrauniversity level.

3. The most authoritative proposals are the SDS (German Socialist Student Union) memorandum on the universities and a reform proposal worked out by a commission of the Association of German Student Bodies (VDS). See also Wolfgang Nitsch et al., *Hochschule in der Demokratie* (Neuwied, 1965).

Chapter 2   Student Protest in the Federal Republic of Germany

1. See Shmuel Noah Eisenstadt, *From Generation to Generation* (Glencoe, 1956), pp. 171 f., as well as Talcott Parsons, "Youth in the Context of American Society," in *Youth: Change and Challenge,* Erik H. Erikson, ed. (New York, 1963), pp. 93 f.

2. Seymour Martin Lipset and Philip G. Altbach, "Student Politics and Higher Education in the U.S.A.," in *Student Politics,* Seymour Martin Lipset, ed. (New York, 1967), p. 243; see also pp. 199 f.

3. See the documents in Hal Draper, *Berkeley, the New Student Revolt* (New York, 1965), and Seymour Martin Lipset and Sheldon S. Wolin, *The Berkeley Student Revolt* (Garden City, 1965).

4. See J. Hager and H. Haüssermann, *Die Rebellen von Berlin* (Cologne, 1967), pp. 26 ff.

5. See Wolfgang Nitsch et al., *Hochschule in der Demokratie*, and the VDS report "Studenten und die neue Universität," 1962.

6. Kurt Sontheimer, "Studenten auf Kollisionkurs," in *Merkur*, No. 233, pp. 701 f.

7. B. Larsson, *Demonstrationen: Ein Berliner Modell* (Berlin, 1967).

8. Joseph Ben-David and Randall Collins, "Academic Freedom and Student Politics," in Lipset, *Student Politics*.

Chapter 3   The Movement in Germany: A Critical Analysis

1. See Claus Offe, "Politische Herrschaft und Klassenstrukturen," in *Politikwissenschaft*, Gisela Kress and Dieter Senghaas, eds. (Frankfurt am Main, 1969).

2. For bibliography see Kenneth Keniston, "The Sources of Student Discontent," in *Journal of Social Issues*, 23:3, pp. 108 ff., and W. A. Watts and D. Wittaker, "Profile of a Non-Conformist Youth Culture," in *Sociology of Education*, 41:1, pp. 178 ff.

3. See Peter L. Berger, *The Sacred Canopy* (New York, 1967) and the essay "Technology and Science as 'Ideology,'" pp. 81–122 below.

Chapter 4   Technical Progress and the Social Life-World

1. Aldous Huxley, *Literature and Science* (New York, 1963), p. 8.

2. *Ibid.*

3. *Ibid.*, p. 9.

4. *Ibid.*, p. 107.

Chapter 5   The Scientization of Politics and Public Opinion

1. Max Weber, *Gesammelte Politischen Schriften*, 2d ed., (Tübingen, 1958), pp. 308 ff.

2. Jacques Ellul, *The Technological Society* (New York, 1967); Helmut Schelsky, *Der Mensch in der wissenschaftlichen Zivilisation* (Cologne-Opladen, 1961).

3. See Helmut Krauch, "Wider den technischen Staat," in *Atomzeitalter*, 1961, No. 9, pp. 201 ff.

4. Hans P. Bahrdt, "Helmut Schelskys technischer Staat," in *Atomzeitalter*, 1961, No. 9, pp. 195 ff.; Jürgen Habermas, "Vom sozialen Wandel akademischer Bildung," in *Universitätstage 1963* (Berlin, 1963), pp. 165 ff.

5. Hermann Lübbe, "Zur politischen Theorie der Technokratie," in *Der Staat*, 1:7, p. 21.

6. Schelsky, *op. cit.*, p. 22.

7. Hermann Lübbe, "Die Freiheit der Theorie," in *Archiv für Rechts- und Sozialphilosophie*, 1962, pp. 343 ff.

8. See Helmut Krauch, "Technische Information und öffentliches Bewusstsein," in *Atomzeitalter*, 1963, No. 9, pp. 235 ff.

9. See my study *Strukturwandel der Öffentlichkeit*, 3d ed. (Neuwied, 1968).

10. Derek J. de Solla Price, *Science Since Babylon* (New Haven, 1961) and *Little Science, Big Science* (New York, 1963). See also Hans P. Dreitzel, "Wachstum und Fortschritt der Wissenschaft," in *Atomzeitalter*, 1963, No. 11, p. 289.

11. Krauch, "Technische Information," p. 238.

12. *Strategie heute* (Frankfurt am Main, 1962), especially Chapter XII, pp. 292 ff.

Chapter 6   Technology and Science as "Ideology"

1. Herbert Marcuse, "Industrialization and Capitalism in the Work of Max Weber," in *Negations: Essays in Critical Theory*, with translations from the German by Jeremy J. Shapiro (Boston, 1968), pp. 223 f.

2. Herbert Marcuse, "Freedom and Freud's Theory of the Instincts," in *Five Lectures,* translations by Jeremy J. Shapiro and Shierry M. Weber (Boston, 1970), p. 16.

3. *Ibid.,* p. 3.

4. *Ibid.*

5. *Ibid.*

6. Herbert Marcuse, *One-Dimensional Man* (Boston, 1964).

7. *Ibid.,* pp. 166 f.

8. *Ibid.,* p. 236.

9. "This law expresses an intratechnical occurrence, a process that man has not willed as a whole. Rather, it takes place, as it were, behind his back, instinctively extending through the entire history of human culture. Furthermore, in accordance with this law, technology cannot evolve beyond the stage of the greatest possible automation, for there are no further specifiable regions of human achievement that could be objectified." Arnold Gehlen, "Anthropologische Ansicht der Technik," in *Technik im technischen Zeitalter,* Hans Freyer *et al.,* eds. (Düsseldorf, 1965).

10. Marcuse, *One-Dimensional Man,* p. 235.

11. *Ibid.,* p. 154.

12. On the context of these concepts in the history of philosophy, see my contribution to the *Festschrift* for Karl Löwith: "Arbeit und Interaktion: Bemerkungen zu Hegels Jenenser Realphilosophie," in *Natur und Geschichte. Karl Löwith zum 70. Geburtstag,* Hermann Braun and Manfred Riedel, eds. (Stuttgart, 1967). This essay is reprinted in *Technik und Wissenschaft als 'Ideologie'* (Frankfurt am Main, 1968) and will appear in English in *Theory and Practice,* to be published by Beacon Press.

13. Gerhard E. Lenski, *Power and Privilege: A Theory of Social Stratification* (New York, 1966).

14. See Peter L. Berger, *The Sacred Canopy* (New York, 1967).

15. See my study *Erkenntnis und Interesse* (Frankfurt am Main, 1968), to be published by Beacon Press as *Cognition and Human Interests.*

16. See Leo Strauss, *Natural Right and History* (Chicago, 1963); C. B. MacPherson, *The Political Theory of Possessive Individualism* (London, 1962); and Jürgen Habermas, "Die klassische Lehre von der Politik in ihrem Verhältnis zur Sozialphilosophie," in *Theorie und Praxis,* 2d ed. (Neuwied, 1967), to appear in *Theory and Practice.*

17. See Jürgen Habermas, "Naturrecht und Revolution," in *Theorie und Praxis.*

18. Claus Offe, "Politische Herrschaft und Klassenstrukturen," in Gisela Kress and Dieter Senghaas, eds., *Politikwissenschaft* (Frankfurt am Main, 1969). The quotation in the text is from the original manuscript, which differs in formulation from the published text.

19. The most recent explication of this is Eugen Löbl, *Geistige Arbeit—die wahre Quelle des Reichtums,* translated from the Czech by Leopold Grünwald (Vienna, 1968).

20. See Helmut Schelsky, *Der Mensch in der wissenschaftlichen Zivilisation* (Cologne-Opladen, 1961); Jacques Ellul, *The Technological Society* (New York, 1967); and Arnold Gehlen, "Über kulturelle Kristallisationen," in *Studien zur Anthropologie und Soziologie (Berlin, 1963),* and "Über kulturelle Evolution," in *Die Philosophie und die Frage nach dem Fortschritt,* M. Hahn and F. Wiedmann, eds. (Munich, 1964).

21. To my knowledge there are no empirical studies concerned specifically with the propagation of this background ideology. We are dependent on extrapolations from the findings of other investigations.

22. Offe, op. cit.

23. See my essay "Erkenntnis und Interesse" in *Technik und Wissenschaft als 'Ideologie.'* It will appear in English as an appendix to *Cognition and Human Interests.*

24. Herman Kahn and Anthony J. Wiener, "The Next Thirty-Three Years: A Framework for Speculation," in *Toward the Year 2000: Work in Progress,* Daniel Bell, ed. (Boston, 1969), pp. 80 f.

25. Seymour Martin Lipset and Philip G. Altbach, "Student Politics and Higher Education in the U.S.A.," in *Student Politics,* Seymour Martin Lipset, ed. (New York, 1967); Richard W. Flacks, "The Liberated Generation: An Exploration of the Roots of Student Protest," in *Journal of Social Issues,* 23:3, pp. 52–75; and Kenneth Keniston, "The Sources of Student Dissent," *ibid.,* pp. 108 ff.

26. In Flacks' words, "Activists are more radical than their parents; but activists' parents are decidedly more liberal than others of their status. . . . Activism is related to a complex of values, not ostensibly political, shared by both the students and their parents. . . . Activists' parents are more 'permissive' than parents of non-activists."

27. See Robert L. Heilbroner, *The Limits of American Capitalism* (New York, 1966).

Index